CRAVE
NEW YORK CITY

The Urban Girl's Manifesto

D1312072

Melody Biringer

CRAVE New York City: The Urban Girl's Manifesto

A publication of The CRAVE Company
1805 12th Ave W #A
Seattle WA 98119
206.282.0173

thecravecompany.com/nyc
twitter.com/cravenyc
facebook.com/cravenyc

While every effort was made to ensure the accuracy of the information, details are subject to change so please call ahead. Neither The CRAVE Company nor CRAVE NYC shall be responsible for any consequences arising from the publication or use.

All editorial content in this publication is the sole opinion of CRAVE NYC and our contributing writers. No fees or services were rendered in exchange for inclusion in this publication.

Printed in the United States of America

ISBN 978-0-9832047-8-7
First Edition
June 2011
$19.95 USD

The Urban Girl's Manifesto

We CRAVE Community.

At CRAVE New York City we believe in acknowledging, celebrating and passionately supporting local businesses. We know that, when encouraged to thrive, neighborhood establishments enhance communities and provide rich experiences not usually encountered in mass-market. By introducing you to the savvy businesswomen in this guide, we hope that CRAVE New York City will help inspire your own inner entrepreneur.

We CRAVE Adventure.

We could all use a getaway, and at CRAVE New York City we believe that you don't need to be a jet-setter to have a little adventure. There's so much to do and explore right in your own backyard. We encourage you to break your routine, to venture away from your regular haunts, to visit new businesses, to explore all the funky finds and surprising spots that New York City has to offer. Whether it's to hunt for a birthday gift, indulge in a spa treatment, order a bouquet of flowers or connect with like-minded people, let CRAVE New York City be your guide for a one-of-a-kind hometown adventure.

We CRAVE Quality.

CRAVE New York City is all about quality products and thoughtful service. We know that a satisfying shopping trip requires more than a simple exchange of money for goods, and that a rejuvenating spa date entails more than a quick clip of the cuticles and a swipe of polish. We know you want to come away feeling uplifted, beautiful, excited, relaxed, relieved and, above all, knowing you got the most bang for your buck. We have scoured the city to find the hidden gems, new hot spots and old standbys, all with one thing in common: they're the best of the best!

A Guide to Our Guide

CRAVE New York City is more than a guidebook. It's a savvy, quality-of-lifestyle book devoted entirely to local businesses owned by women. CRAVE New York City will direct you to some of the best local spots—top boutiques, spas, cafés, stylists, fitness studios and more. And we'll introduce you to the inspired, dedicated women behind these exceptional enterprises, for whom creativity, quality, innovation and customer service are paramount.

Not only is CRAVE New York City an intelligent guide for those wanting to know what's happening throughout town, it's a directory for those who value the contributions that spirited businesswomen make to our region.

ASTROSTYLE.COM

astrostyle.com, Twitter: @astrotwins
By appointment only: E 12th St, New York (email astrotwins@astrostyle.com)

Savvy. Empowering. Trustworthy.
The AstroTwins, Tali and Ophira Edut, bring the stars down to earth with savvy and empowering astrological advice. Through their website, columns, books, events and private consultations, they help you unlock your "cosmic code" so you can reach your star-powered potential in all areas of life. They are the official astrologers for Elle.com and MyLifetime.com and have read for celebs including Beyonce and Sting.

Tali and Ophira Edut

Q&A

What are your most popular products or services?
One-on-one readings. Event appearances. Our book *Love Zodiac*, a guide to the men of every sign. Daily, weekly and monthly horoscopes on Astrostyle.com. Sirius radio for our monthly call-in guest spot.

What do you like best about owning a business?
As go-getter Sagittarians and identical twins, we are always motivating each other. We started with a calligraphy biz when we were 8 years old and haven't stopped collaborating since.

What do you CRAVE?
Burning Man, Paris flea markets, turquoise waters. Genuine connections with people. Mini dachshunds. Family time. More great tools for indie publishing.

AVANTGARDE COMMUNICATIONS GROUP

732.385.1714
agcomgroup.com, Twitter: @agcg

Insightful. Sharp. Dedicated.
AvantGarde Communications Group (AGCG) is a firm that delivers expertise in PR, marketing, business development, copywriting and creative solutions. Much like a first-class couture designer, AGCG tailors programs based on needs, objectives and more. So whether you're looking to define an image for your brand or want to spread the word about who you are and what you do, this is who you call on!

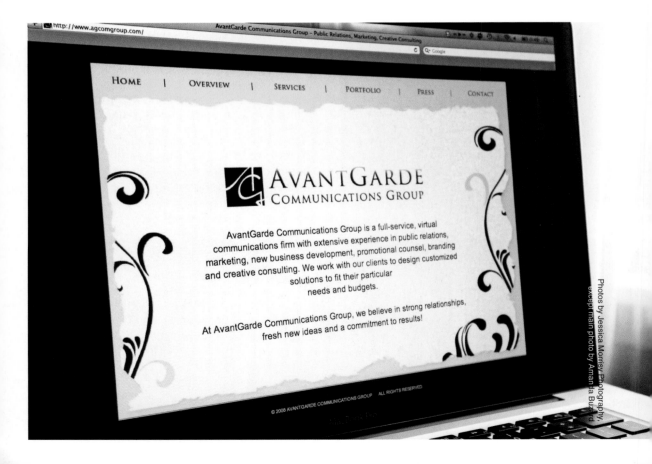

Inna Shamis

Q&A

What tip would you give women who are starting a business?
Be passionate and resilient! And keep this in mind: "There are no mistakes, only lessons. Love yourself, trust your choices, and everything is possible." —Cherie Carter-Scott

What do you like best about owning a business?
I'm the boss! The inherent ability to follow my own instincts. And the license to work with those who ignite my interest.

Who is your role model or mentor?
My mother, who ignited my entrepreneurial spirit and taught me some of those most important lessons: pursue your passion, never give in to fear and if one door closes, a better one opens!

What is your biggest fear?
"The greatest mistake we make is living in constant fear that we will make one." —John Maxwell

What is your motto or theme song?
I have several: Never make a promise you can't keep. Underpromise and overdeliver. Lead, follow or get out of the way.

Erica Kiang
(right)

 # Q&A

What are your most popular products or services?
Antique African beaded necklaces from Ghana and paper robots from Japan.

Who is your role model or mentor?
My mother.

What motivates you on a daily basis?
The constant talent that surrounds me in my industry. I love to see what other stores, designers and creative people are doing.

How do you relax?
Watching bad movies and reading business books on international flights.

What place inspires you and why?
New York. Inspiring things and people are around you all the time. I'm constantly impressed.

BABEL FAIR

260 Elizabeth St, New York, 646.360.3685
babelfair.com, Twitter: @BabelFair

Global. Eccentric. Forward.

Babel Fair is a specialty women's apparel and lifestyle boutique in downtown
Manhattan. Constantly scouring the globe, Babel Fair carries a unique and
constantly changing international assortment. From Japanese denim to
Argentinean leather, Babel Fair offers a rare shopping experience showcasing
talent from around the world. Babel Fair has recently expanded into Babel
Fair Showroom, which provides other retailers with their unique products.

Rachel Venning and
Claire Cavanah

 Q&A

What are your most popular
products or services?
High-end, discreet, rechargeable
vibes from companies such as Lelo,
Jimmyjane, We-Vibe, Je Joue and Fun
Factory; fun and educational workshops;
and a knowledgeable and friendly staff
of trained Sexuality Educators.

What tip would you give women
who are starting a business?
Set things up so monthly expenses are
low—you can grow expense with revenue,
but it puts pressure on you if you have
a big number to make each month.

Who is your role model or mentor?
Ben & Jerry. Just like ours, their business
is about pleasure plus politics.

What motivates you on a daily basis?
Women having more and better orgasms.

Main photo courtesy Babeland, lower left, photos by Barbie Hull Photography, portrait by Sarah Small

Brooklyn

Lower East Side

SoHo

BABELAND

43 Mercer St, New York, 212.966.2120
94 Rivington St, New York, 212.375.1701
462 Bergen St, Brooklyn, 718.638.3820
babeland.com, babeland.tumblr.com, Twitter: @Babeland_NYC

Sexy. Fun. Knowledgeable.
Babeland is the famously friendly sex toy boutique offering top-quality products, a pleasant place to shop, and, most of all, information and encouragement to women who want to explore their sexuality. The popularity of their flagship location in Seattle has led to three stores in New York, plus a thriving and educational website.

17

BABYBITES AND KIDDYBITES

babybites.com, Twitter: @babybites

Social. Educational. Supportive.
Babybites and kiddybites are social and educational communities for moms and moms-to-be. Their mission is to provide advice and support to moms via their events, support groups and resources. They offer many free online services including webinars, original parenting videos by experts, blog talk radio shows, and fresh, informative articles on various parenting topics. They are also known for their premium, mom-generated nanny and babysitter listings.

Laura Deutsch and
Heather Ouida

Q&A

What do you like best about
owning a business?
Being our own boss, being able to choose
amazing people to work with, the challenge
of wearing many hats and the thrill of
building something from the ground up.

Who is your role model or mentor?
Our moms! Being a mom community,
it's only natural that we turn to our
moms for guidance and support. They
help keep things in perspective and
are our biggest cheerleaders.

What motivates you on a daily basis?
Our babybites community. It is because
of our loyal community that we are always
implementing new ways to help moms with
one of the hardest jobs of all—parenting!

Heather Marold
Thomason

 # Q&A

What are your most popular products or services?
Recently we've designed and built many websites using the Wordpress publishing platform. It's an empowering, user-friendly solution for our clients to manage their own website content.

What tip would you give women who are starting a business?
Work hard but be sure to make time for the people and things you love. Maintaining a work-life balance will keep you and your business happy and healthy.

What do you like best about owning a business?
Our clients trust us to define their visual style. I love this responsibility, and feel truly proud when our ideas and creativity contribute to the success of a brand.

BAD FEATHER

badfeather.com, Twitter: @badfeather

Smart. Savvy. Bold.

Bad Feather is a graphic design firm that specializes in identity design and branding as well as website design, strategy and development. Founded in 2008 by a husband-and-wife team with a passion for art, design and technology, Bad Feather works with creative businesses to address their challenges and realize their goals through design.

Miriam Milord

Q&A

What are your most popular products or services?
We specialize in three-dimensional cake sculptures in every imaginable shape from fashion purses to pets, combined with unique cake flavors.

What or who inspired you to start your business?
The lack of cakes that are both beautiful and delicious.

What is your indulgence?
My true indulgence is hot chocolate and shoes; luckily I don't have too much free time to indulge...

What do you CRAVE? In business? In life?
Excitement, satisfaction and happiness. I love to see my clients' faces when they see their cakes for the first time.

BCAKENY

702 Washington Ave, Brooklyn, 347.787.7199
bcakeny.com, Twitter: @bcakeny

Creative. Fresh. Delicious.
BCakeNY is a custom cake-design studio dedicated to creating specialty cakes for every occasion. They transfer your vision into unique and delicious cakes and always bring special attention to your event by creating the most amazing cake that will wow everyone. Their mission is to combine beauty and creativity with the scrumptious taste of homemade cake. *Anything can BCake!*

Portrait and upper middle photo by Jen Huang Photography, main photo and upper left and right photos by BCakeNY

BELATHÉE PHOTOGRAPHY

917.783.3207
belathee.com, Twitter: @belathee

Compassionate. Timeless. Inspired.

Annabel and Dorothée came together in 2003 to launch Belathée Photography. Combining a romantic, timeless quality with a modern, fresh and wonderfully inventive perspective, their work feels delicate and powerful all at once. Annabel and Dorothée love to tell your story by creating a collection of photographs that reflect all of the joy, emotion and atmosphere surrounding you and what you stand for.

Annabel Braithwaite
and Dorothée Brand

 # Q&A

What are your most popular products or services?
While wedding photography is our specialty, our photographic range covers families, children, travel, events and food, as well as fine art.

What tip would you give women who are starting a business?
Follow your goals with fantasy/humor, then bring them to life with sturdy steps in the same direction. Focus on what sets you apart from what is already being offered.

What do you like best about owning a business?
We love having the control of crafting our own style and approach. Being able to connect with our clients directly is very rewarding, as is building long-term relationships.

Wanda Mann

Q&A

What are your most popular products or services?
In addition to showcasing the best destinations for female travelers, The Black Dress Traveler features travel-friendly beauty products, fashion, food and wine.

Who is your role model or mentor?
I inherited my Grandma Bertha's sense of adventure. She left home at a young age to pursue a singing career and landed a recording contract. She wasn't afraid to shine.

What is your motto or theme song?
"Travel is more than the seeing of sights; it is a change that goes on, deep and permanent, in the ideas of living." —Miriam Beard

What place inspires you and why?
My hometown, NYC, never ceases to inspire me. NYC is energized by people from all over the world who come here in pursuit of a dream.

What do you CRAVE?
Exploring new places, meeting people full of laughter and light, food that is made with passion, wine that tells a story and the perfect little black dress!

THE BLACK DRESS TRAVELER

212.726.2210
blackdresstraveler.com, Twitter: @blackdressdiva

Vivacious. Stylish. Savvy.
The Black Dress Traveler is a dynamic website that provides adventurous fashionistas with the information needed to travel the world in style. From where to go to what to wear, The Black Dress Traveler provides travel information from a female perspective. Adventure is always in fashion and The Black Dress Traveler encourages readers to be prepared with a little black dress whenever they travel.

BUMP BROOKLYN

464 Bergen St, Brooklyn, 718.638.1960
bumpbrooklyn.com

Contemporary. Chic. Comfortable.

Bump's motto is simple: "Give up wine, sushi, coffee—not fashion." Bump was founded in 2007 by two fashion-conscious moms who were surprised by the lack of stylish options for pregnant women and new moms in a borough bustling with babies. Bump is a boutique designed for the urban woman who is not willing to give up her sense of style while pregnant or nursing.

Hannah Macdonald and
SaSaDi Oduns

Q&A

What are your most popular products or services?
Beautiful dresses, nursing bras, J Brand jeans, Basq skin care, BellaBands, personalized jewelry, and storksak diaper bags.

People may be surprised to know...
Bump carries a number of wonderful contemporary designers like Susana Monaco, Line and Yumi Kim, who feature styles that can be worn during pregnancy and long afterward.

What is your indulgence?
Tres Belle facials, travel, clothes, shoes, good food and wine, ice cream and Brooklyn Flea weekends.

Allison MacCullough O'Neill

Q&A

What are your most popular
products or services?
Our most popular items are onesies, custom
blankets and stuffed animals; our concierge
is our most popular service. We take all
the work out of sending the perfect gift!

What tip would you give women
who are starting a business?
Identify your competitive advantage and
with every dollar you're tempted to spend
(inventory, marketing, anything), think
about whether or not it will help solidify that
advantage and make decisions accordingly.

What is do you like best about
owning a business?
When I am walking around NYC and I
randomly spot someone carrying a Bundle
shopping bag, it is the most amazing thing!

BUNDLE
CHILDREN'S BOUTIQUE

128 Thompson St, New York, 212.982.9465
bundlenyc.com

Drool-worthy. Friendly. Adorable.
Bundle is a chic, new children's boutique offering a beautiful selection
of clothing and gifts for children from newborn through age 6. A favorite
store of many style-savvy New Yorkers, as well as A-list celebrities and
stylists, Bundle takes great pride in selecting only the finest products
available and in keeping merchandise reasonably priced.

Photos by Erin Leigh

SoHo

CARLI BEARDSLEY ATELIER

917.576.7491
carli.custom@gmail.com

Discreet. Eclectic. Inventive.
Carli Beardsley is a concierge tailor and artisanal stitcher for the home. Incorporating her 20 years' experience as a theatrical costumer and set decorator, Carli can help you revamp your wardrobe or stitch up a gorgeous textile confection to decorate your favorite old chair! Put her attention to detail and discreet manner to work for you. Have sewing machine—will travel!

Carli Beardsley

Q&A

What are your most popular products or services?
Concierge tailoring—fittings at home or the office. Wardrobe styling. Costume production. Soft properties production for stage and film. Interior decorating and color consultation. Home staging for real estate sales.

What tip would you give women who are starting a business?
Be ready to work hard at your craft or skill *and* take care of the nuts and bolts of business. Doing paperwork isn't sexy, but it keeps you moving forward!

Who is your role model or mentor?
My dad. He taught me to not fear new things—whether it be gaining a new skill or getting advice to become better at what I already know!

The Decorista with embroidery by LuxuryMonograms.com
photographed by Belathée Photography

What place inspires you and why?

" New York! No place is more inspirational, artful and upbeat. This city is amazing. "

Francine Rivera of Soapology

CAUSEY
CONTEMPORARY

92 Wythe Ave, Brooklyn, 718.218.8939
causeycontemporary.com

Exquisite. Art-filled. Contemporary.
Causey Contemporary, an 11-year veteran of the Williamsburg art gallery scene, cultivates and represents contemporary artists from their emergence through their maturity. They are dedicated to helping collectors understand and enjoy their artworks within historical, cultural and social contexts. Their mission is to nourish dialogue and relationships between artists, collectors and curators via exhibitions, studio tours and special events.

Q&A

What are your most popular products or services?
Paintings by Elise Freda or Alexis Portilla, drawings by Norman Mooney or Kevin Bourgeois, and sculptures by Steven Dobbin or John Clement.

What or who inspired you to start your business?
The artists I met who create daily because they are passionate about the art they make and are often in need of representation that has their best interest in mind.

Who is your role model or mentor?
My role models are women like Peggy Guggenheim and later, Mary Boone. My mentor is an elderly sculptor, Sy Gresser, who has seen and participated in the art world since the 1950s along with my father, who was an entrepreneur in his own right.

How do you spend your free time?
Reading voraciously, writing poetry, walking with my husband, gardening, visiting other art exhibitions, traveling and enjoying great wines with friends and family.

Where is your favorite place to go with your girlfriends?
D.O.C. wine bar, the Richardson and Baci and Abbraci in Williamsburg.

Williamsburg

Tracy Causey-Jeffery

CENTER OF FEMALE EMPOWERMENT

347.497.DIVA (3482)
lusciouslifestylediva.com, Twitter: @shoshi

Sexy. Sensual. Spiritual.
Yolanda Shoshana ("Shoshi") is the creator of a lifestyle company for women that swirls sexuality, sensuality and spirituality, which has made her known as the "Luscious Lifestyle Diva." Her passion is helping women leave behind the good-enough life and live lusciously. She brings back the virtues of the courtesans, taps into the senses and plays with the art of seduction.

Yolanda Shoshana

Q&A

What or who inspired you to start your business?
Women who want more out of life but did not know how to get it. That's where I come in.

Who is your role model or mentor?
Ali Brown. She is a fierce force, and I strive to be as savvy a businesswoman as she is.

What business mistake have you made that you will not repeat?
My big mistake was not listening to my intuition; now it is where I go to first.

Where is your favorite place to go with your girlfriends?
I love going to Yankee Stadium. Not only do I get to see my favorite team, there's also a buffet of men.

Sydney Price

Q&A

What tip would you give women who are starting a business?
Have a clear and complete vision of what you want to create, plan every step to reach your goals and never compromise on what is important to you.

What do you like best about owning a business?
It is a huge creative outlet for me. I am able to bring my dreams to reality every day, constantly enhancing and refining the environment and the visitor experience.

Who is your role model or mentor?
Mark Kalow taught me to seek good advice and the importance of balancing inspiration with stability. John Wilczak showed me that unwavering focus and determination will ultimately lead to success.

CITY TREEHOUSE

129A W 20th St, Ground Floor, New York, 212.255.2050
citytreehouse.com, Twitter: @citytreehouse

Fun. Educational. Nurturing.
City Treehouse is home to the largest indoor water-play area in NYC and
is also an oasis of fun and learning. Families enjoy drop-in play, birthday
parties, classes and special events in an environment filled with trees, plants
and laughter. It is no wonder that City Treehouse is recognized as Best
of New York by Nickelodeon, *New York Magazine* and Urban Baby!

Chelsea

CLINTON ST. BAKING CO.

4 Clinton St, New York, 646.602.6263
clintonstreetbaking.com

COMMUNITY FOOD & JUICE

2893 Broadway (at 112th St), New York, 212.665.2800
communityrestaurant.com

CLINTON ST. CATERING

4 Clinton St, New York, 646.602.6263
clintonstreetbaking.com, dede@clintonstreetbaking.com

Hip. Homey. Delicious.
The Clinton St. Baking Company is one of the hottest brunch spots in a city
obsessed with brunch. A tiny 32-seat eatery on Manhattan's trendy Lower East Side,
the restaurant draws around-the-block lines of devoted fans who come from far
and wide (including a large contingent from Japan) to sample fresh baked goods,
hearty omelets, sugar-cured bacon and light-as-air pancakes with maple butter.

Community Food & Juice

Photos by Belathée Photography

DeDe Lahman

Q&A

What tip would you give women who are starting a business?
Be assertive. Have more than a wing and a prayer—your numbers need to make sense beyond the great idea. Write down concrete goals. Never waver from your brand.

Who is your role model or mentor?
My grandmother was a doctor with a private practice. She was strong and focused and accumulated her own wealth.

What motivates you on a daily basis?
Making money. Being creative. Serving guests. Finding new and exciting projects. Marketing the business.

What place inspires you and why?
NYC, baby! Best city to live and work in. Cultures, people, food, smells, architecture, sounds, wheels, shops—we have it all here.

COLOR OUR WORLD

265 E 66th St, New York, 212.249.0090
colorourworld.com

Enriching. Colorful. Homey.

Gillian C. Rose, an interior and color designer, creator/owner of Color Our World
can help you with your space, your colors, your feeling of well-being. Using a unique
blend of color psychology and the most exquisite color palette, Color Our World
will create you, in color! If your home or office does not represent you, they can!
Their patented process delves into the hows and whys, through personality and
color, to create the surrounding that you want to be immersed in every day.

Portrait, main and upper left photos by Michael Mundy,
upper middle and right photos by Gillan Rose

Gillian C. Rose

 Q&A

What are your most popular
products or services?
Paint colors that create a sense
of well-being and reflect who
they are created for.

People may be surprised to know...
Pale colors are not usually
soothing and relaxing.

How do you spend your free time?
Going to museums. Relaxing over
a homemade meal with friends.

What is your indulgence?
Vintage colored glass.

What do you CRAVE? In business? In life?
Bringing the perfect color to each
and every person and becoming
an international company.

CURIOUS LIGHT

917.447.4864
curiouslight.com, Twitter: @curiouslt

Creative. Unique. Professional.
Curious Light designs and builds high-quality, affordable and stylish websites that
will give your small business a big online presence. Owner Nadine Gilden is a
seasoned website and graphic designer, with more than 12 years of experience.
Curious Light also assists companies in creating their marketing materials such
as WordPress blogs, email newsletters, business cards and Twitter pages.

Photos by Sofia Negron Photography

Nadine Gilden

Q&A

What are your most popular products or services?
E-commerce and information sites, email newsletters and business cards.

People may be surprised to know...
The name Curious Light came from Curious George and my love of stained glass.

What or who inspired you to start your business?
The desire to work with a variety of clients on many different kinds of projects.

What business mistake have you made that you will not repeat?
Not trusting my instincts. If alarm bells go off, pay attention to them!

How do you spend your free time?
With family and friends enjoying all that New York has to offer— shows, shopping, restaurants...

Where is your favorite place to go with your girlfriends?
I love a good brunch, so anywhere that has one!

What do you CRAVE? In business? In life?
Projects that both challenge and inspire me. To be happy and appreciate what I have instead of wishing for what I don't have.

Main photo by Bree Michael Warner Photography, portrait by Jen Huang Photography, lower left photo by Spencer Lum of 5 West Studios, lower middle photo by Gordon Studio Photography, lower right photo by Jensen Studio Weddings

CURTAIN UP EVENTS, INC.

By appointment only, 212.781.6390
curtainupevents.com, Twitter: @curtainupevents

Innovative. Savvy. Chic.

Curtain Up Events (CUE) provides planning and coordination services for intimate to large affairs, applying the unique insights of a professional theatrical background to produce unforgettably distinctive events. From initial concept to budgeting, production and execution, CUE works with its clients to realize the particular occasion they have envisioned or can provide full creative direction.

Danielle Bobish

Q&A

What tip would you give women who are starting a business?
Treat everyone who works for/with you with respect. I could never do what I do without my team. It may seem obvious, but you'd be surprised how many people forget.

What motivates you on a daily basis?
My clients. There's nothing better than seeing the end result of all of your hard work and then hearing from your client that it exceeded their expectations.

What is your motto or theme song?
We have two slogans: "Dramatic events... without all the 'drama'" and "Make sure your events happen on CUE."

What place inspires you and why?
Florence, Italy. It's such an amazing place to be. They really know how to appreciate life there. Food, wine, friends, family...

Ashlina Kaposta

Q&A

What do you like best about owning a business?
I love that I had a wild idea and it worked! It's so fulfilling to be doing what I absolutely love to do, every day.

What motivates you on a daily basis?
My passion for interiors and joie de vivre. Anything from a flower to amazing architecture can give me that boost of motivation to create something new.

What is your motto or theme song?
"I am going to make everything around me more beautiful. That will be my life." —Elsie de Wolfe

What place inspires you and why?
NYC! From the NY Library to Central Park, I am constantly inspired by the art and architecture of this city. Not to mention the fashion, it's intoxicating!

THE DECORISTA

thedecorista.com, ashlinakaposta.com, Twitter: @thedecorista

Inspired. Vibrant. Dynamic.
The Decorista provides fully customizable design experiences, from full-scale interiors to virtual decorating services around the globe. Ashlina's skills have lended themselves to styling successful ad campaigns and cultivating one-of-a-kind looks that have landed her work in several publications. Her hands-on approach ensures complete client satisfaction. The Decorista's widely acclaimed design blog provides daily inspiration to thousands of readers.

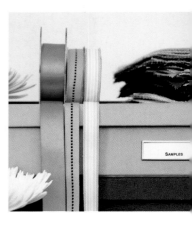

Dawn Van Dyke and
Melisa Dreyfuss

Q&A

What do you like best about
owning a business?
Personal connections. We are there
for one of the most stressful and
magical days of our clients' lives,
and we do not take that lightly!

What motivates you on a daily basis?
The industry! We are surrounded by
immense talent that inspires us to continue
creating, dreaming and designing.

How do you relax?
We would love to say "a good book" or
"a day at the spa" but let's be honest, we
relax with a glass of wine and trashy TV!

What place inspires you and why?
Anywhere natural, whether it is a
beach, forest or desert. Living in a
city can make you crave the organic
elements and color palettes of nature.

DM EVENTS

646.530.3440
dmeventsny.com, Twitter: @DMeventsny

Whimsical. Passionate. Detailed.
DM Events is a boutique-style event planning and design company. These ladies love what they do and it shows! From the linen to the flowers... and every color swatch in between... they will help you create a design that reflects your own fabulous style! Services include full, partial and day-of event coordination packages as well as custom designs and floral packages. *Happy planning!*

Photos by Sara & Sarma Photography

Main photo by Lloyd C. Kirkland, lower right photos by Gwen Rodgers, portrait by Sofia Negron Photography

DOCE VIDA FITNESS WEAR

docevidafitness.com, Twitter: @docevidafitness

Stylish. Slimming. Super moisture-wicking.
Doce Vida was created under the mantra that every woman should feel fabulous about her body no matter what size or shape she may be. Their flattering fits feature an ultrasoft, instantly slimming 12 percent four-way stretch fabric that feels like butter against your skin as it wicks away moisture, so you can keep your body moving in comfort and style.

Jordan Goffi and Lisa Pidge

Q&A

What or who inspired you to start your business?
Growing up in athletic families who basically lived in workout clothes, we felt they never fit well. We were inspired to create a line that flattered a woman's body. Our fashion and yoga teacher backgrounds helped us to create stylish, functional, long-lasting fitness wear.

What is your indulgence?
We love spa treatments! We are advocates for a whole health lifestyle.

What do you CRAVE? In business? In life?
In business, we crave for all women to experience the difference Doce Vida makes in their workouts. We love hearing from happy customers about how Doce Vida makes them feel. In life, we crave health and being surrounded by positive people.

ELIZABETH CHARLES

639 1/2 Hudson St, New York, 212.243.3201
elizabeth-charles.com, Twitter: @MsCharles

Chic. Authentic. Personalized.
Elizabeth Charles is a high-end multibrand boutique located in New York and San
Francisco that carries an unparalleled selection of coveted and hard-to-find women's
clothing and accessories from around the world including Carven, Isabel Marant and
Preen. The boutique's originality, unique mix of constantly evolving merchandise
and highly personalized service have attracted a loyal and discerning clientele.

Photos by Emily DeWan Photography

Elizabeth
Charles

Q&A

**What tip would you give women
who are starting a business?**
Keep refining your business plan by
incorporating feedback and primary
research and then *do it*! Dreams need
to be executed to become a reality.

**What do you like best about
owning a business?**
It doesn't feel like work, and I get to read
magazines and shop for a living! I get a lot
of satisfaction out of watching my business
grow and become more successful.

What motivates you on a daily basis?
I love the fashion industry and I find it
fascinating from many aspects: trends,
business, consumers and designers. It's a
constant game that keeps me on my toes.

What is your motto or theme song?
You can do whatever you put your mind to.

West Village

Photos by Tracy Toler

ELKE VON FREUDENBERG

1140 Broadway, Ste 906, New York, 917.475.6845
themodelbrow.com, Twitter: @TheModelBrow

Fashionable. Trendy. Stylish.
Celebrity eyebrow specialist Elke Von Freudenberg is considered one of the
best eyebrow shaping experts in New York, specializing in fixing and reshaping
brows that are uneven, badly designed or in the process of growing in.

Elke Von Freudenberg

Q&A

What are your most popular
products or services?
Our Clear Brow Ware, a clear water gel
that grooms and gives a glossy sheen
to brows, sells out constantly. That and
our Model Brow Shaping Service.

People may be surprised to know...
I've been doing eyebrows
since I was 16 years old.

What or who inspired you to
start your business?
Seeing that women felt they had no
say during the experience of getting
their eyebrows shaped, I knew there
had to be a way to offer a better client
consultation as well as experience.

Who is your role model or mentor?
My father. He taught me to be honest,
fair and to treat everyone with respect.

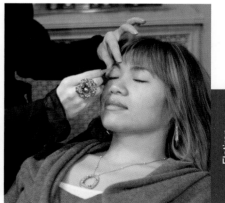

Flatiron

Skin by Kyra photographed by Emily DeWan Photography

What tip would you give women
who are starting a business?

" Have a clear and complete
vision of what you want
to create, plan every step
to reach your goals and
never compromise on what
is important to you. "

Sydney Price of City Treehouse

EMILY DEWAN PHOTOGRAPHY, INC.

917.620.5111
emilydewan.com, Twitter: @emilydewan

Relaxing. Captivating. Timeless.
Emily adores capturing the precious moments of children's lives: holding a parent's hand, cuddling the family pet, playing with siblings and exploring the world around them. She loves to interact with children while photographing their adorable faces. The world is her studio! She'll come to your house, meet you at your favorite neighborhood spot or join you anywhere else you'd like to explore.

Photos by Emily DeWan Photography, except portrait by E. Leigh Photography

Emily DeWan

 Q&A

What are your most popular
products or services?
My clients love the opportunity to be
themselves and have fun during their
portrait sessions. I love putting together
a fine art album to showcase the
relationships between family members.

What is your favorite part about
owning a business?
The ability to create my own road map in life.

How do you relax?
Biking around the city or swing dancing.

What place inspires you and why?
Iceland: I visited the northern part of
the country a few years ago and was
struck by its barely touched beauty.

Patricia Helding

Q&A

What are your most popular
products or services?
The Fat Witch Baby is our most popular
product. It's small but packs just enough
chocolate punch to be satisfying.

What is your biggest fear?
Getting overwhelmed with all the
projects there are to accomplish.

What motivates you on a daily basis?
The business itself. It's exciting
to run something.

What place inspires you and why?
The Metropolitan Museum of Art in NYC
is a source of constant inspiration. Every
work of art was done with passion.

What do you CRAVE?
A long weekend at a fabulous spa.

FAT WITCH BAKERY

75 9th Ave, New York, 212.807.1335
fatwitch.com, Twitter: @fatwitch.com

Fresh. Sassy. Delicious.
Fat Witch is a local brownie bakery. Fat Witch bakes just like you do at
home. The only difference is they bake more pans! Only natural ingredients
are put into these scrumptious chocolate bars, along with a lot of love.
Fat Witch has a shop inside the Chelsea Market and their brownies can
be found in numerous gourmet stores in Manhattan and online.

Photos by Emily DeVan Photography

Chelsea

Sarah and Jenifer Caplan

Q&A

What are your most popular products or services?
Footzyrolls' most popular style is the Sparkle Toe collection, which is the regular everyday shoe with a little glitz at the tip of each of the shoes.

What motivates you on a daily basis?
Satisfaction from happy customers and retail accounts and being able to talk on a daily basis about the product that we created.

What place inspires you and why?
Bergdorf Goodman, because the store and clothes are so beautiful and the customer service is fantastic.

What do you CRAVE?
Bloomingdales' frozen yogurt, attention from good-looking men, Chanel bags/shoes and always being able to get a cab in NYC.

Photos by E.Leigh Photography

FOOTZYROLLS

646.827.0673
footzyrolls.com, Twitter: @footzyrolls

Chic. Compact. Practical.
Footzyrolls was founded by two sisters because they wanted to look fashionable, but couldn't take the pain of the heels they insisted on wearing. Footzyrolls allow women to wear high heels and keep a fashionable walkable street shoe small enough to fit in any handbag.

FRIENDS OF JODI

917.941.5698
friendsofjodi.com, Twitter: @FriendsOfJodi

Strategic. Social. Inspirational.

Friends Of Jodi is a network of colleagues and friends that Jodi Brockington connects professionally and socially. It is also a brand and a blog, which consists of a collection of ideas, commentary and occasional rants about marketing and branding through actions, philanthropy, business, corporate social responsibility and related topics. Consisting of both original and linked content, FOJ strives to provide its audience, clients and community with information to provoke thought, new ideas and increased effectiveness.

NIARA CONSULTING

917.941.5698
niaraconsulting.com

Reliable. Innovative. Energetic.

Jodi Brockington helps clients figure out the career moves, dreams and goals that are right for them. Additionally, she is able to set up exploratory meetings and interviews with professionals in the fields you believe you want to enter, as well as with executive search firms and HR representatives that actually do the hiring and placements. If you are planning to leave your job to become an entrepreneur or are one already, Jodi can also help you plan, explore and connect you to other people, resources and services that will help you get your business to a better place or up and running quickly.

Jodi Brockington

 **Q&A**

What are your most popular products or services?
Social media and business development, consulting, brand building, strategic marketing and sponsorship, connecting/networking, and events with a cause.

What tip would you give women who are starting a business?
Network. Network. Network. You have to do the things that no one else wants to do—that's how you stand out. It's important to realize the power of relationship building.

Who is your role model or mentor?
I have many, but my mother is at the top of the list. She taught me to take the time to help others; especially women.

What motivates you on a daily basis?
My biggest motivators are my FOJs and my family. They support me and always give me a reality check when I need it.

What is your motto or theme song?
"Golden" by Jill Scott. I feel I embody the lyrics to the song and live my life to the fullest.

What place inspires you and why?
The beach—the way the water seems to go on for eternity, the colors, the salt water smell, the crashing waves... it's always changing, but yet always staying the same.

FSL COSMETICS

fslcosmetics.com, Twitter: @FSLCosmetics

Natural. Sexy. Stylish.

FSL Cosmetics is a natural and eco-friendly brand of lipsticks and lip glosses. FSL stands for "Feel good, Smell good, Look good." Each lipstick and lip gloss consists of high-quality botanicals, exotic Brazilian fruits, antioxidants and vitamins. Kimberly Riley is the chemical engineer/cosmetic chemist behind the buzzworthy brand and will continue to use nature's treasures in ways that revolutionize and enhance beauty worldwide.

Photos by Emily DeVan Photography

Kimberly Riley

Q&A

What are your most popular products or services?
Popular colors: Purple Luv (exotic purple with a luscious white-chocolate scent), Pink Colada (neutral pink with a piña colada scent) and Seduction (sexy red with delicious chocolate aromas).

What tip would you give women who are starting a business?
Make sure you do your research, save money, and build your network.

What do you like best about owning a business?
I am my own boss, I can build my business at my own pace, and I can let my creativity run freely.

How do you relax?
Sleep and travel. I love visiting the Caribbean and my hometown, New Orleans.

Katie Shea and Susie Levitt

Q&A

What are your most popular products or services?
CitySlips, foldable, portable ballet flats for the well-heeled gal on the go, and AfterSoles, rollable ballet flats for the dance-floor diva.

People may be surprised to know...
We are 23 years old and started our business out of our dorm room at NYU!

Who is your role model or mentor?
Both of us come from entrepreneurial families. Our fathers were small business owners, and growing up, we saw everything they did on a day-to-day basis.

How do you spend your free time?
We are big believers in working hard and playing hard. When we aren't working, we spend time with our friends and families.

FUNK-TIONAL FOOTWEAR

212.279.2466 x205
cityslips.com, aftersoles.com, Twitter: @cityslips, Twitter: @aftersoles

Innovative. Intelligent. Irresistible.
FUNK-tional Footwear is an up-and-coming women's lifestyle company
dedicated to creating products with both fashion and function in mind.
Within a year of starting the company, Katie and Susie successfully
brought their first patent-pending item to market. CitySlips are now
available at Dillard's, Neiman Marcus and over 1,000 specialty shops
worldwide. AfterSoles can be found nationwide at Bed Bath & Beyond.

GABRIELLE BERNSTEIN

gabbyb.tv, Twitter: @gabbybernstein

Spirited. Fun. Transformational.

Featured in the *New York Times* Sunday Styles section as the next-generation guru, speaker and author, Gabrielle Bernstein is expanding the lexicon for the future. Gabrielle is a #1 best-selling author of the book *Add More ~ing to Your Life*. In September 2011, Gabrielle launches her second book titled *Spirit Junkie: A Radical Road to Self-Love and Miracles*. (Both books published by Random House.) Gabrielle is also the founder of HerFuture.com. For Gabrielle's free meditations visit Gabbyb.tv.

Gabrielle
Bernstein

Q&A

What are your most popular products or services?
My book, *Add More ~ing to Your Life: A Hip Guide to Happiness*. My monthly lectures and four-week workshops.

What tip would you give women who are starting a business?
Make sure you believe in it. Nothing can manifest into success unless you truly believe it can.

What do you like best about owning a business?
I can wear my gym clothes all day. I have always been self-employed so I don't know any other way.

What motivates you on a daily basis?
I am motivated to spread my message to the masses. My mission is to help transform perceptions so you can experience miracles.

What is your motto or theme song?
Your intentions create your reality.

What place inspires you and why?
The Omega Institute because their mission is to inspire others through their empowering workshops.

GER-NIS INTERNATIONAL

540 President St, Ste 2E, Brooklyn, 718.789.2880
ger-nis.com, Twitter: @GerNisInt

Educational. Local. Sustainable.

Ger-Nis specializes in cooking and education classes for adults and children; promoting healthy eating and living habits through hands-on and lecture-style classroom environments. They are a passionate advocate of organic and fair-trade communities from all around the world and are committed to supporting local chefs, farmers and artisans in our own backyard.

Nissa Pierson

 # Q&A

What tip would you give women who are starting a business?
Be a business*woman*, not a business*man*! Be brave, use your instincts and trust your judgment. Have a few business-savvy advisers or friends to use as a sounding board!

What do you like best about owning a business?
Freedom to bring my own creative ideas to fruition. Bringing my dog to work with me every day is also a big plus!

What motivates you on a daily basis?
Creativity. Children. Traveling to see and experience other people and cultures around the world.

GIRLS WRITE NOW

247 W 37th St, Ste 1800, New York, 212.336.9330
girlswritenow.org, Twitter: @girlswritenow

Supportive. Inspiring. Life-changing.
Girls Write Now is the first organization in the US to combine mentoring and writing
instruction within the context of all-girls programming. Since 1998, they've provided a
supportive environment for more than 3,500 at-risk girls to expand their natural talents,
develop independent voices, and build confidence in making healthy choices in school,
work and life. One hundred percent of GWN's seniors graduate and move on to college.

Main photo by Meghan Hickey, portrait and
upper left and middle photos by Bellathée
Photography, upper right photo by Jen Chu

Maya Nussbaum

Q&A

What are your most popular products or services?
The Mentoring Program matches girls with professional women writers for weekly meetings, monthly workshops and public readings each spring. Girls College Bound brings college essay-writing clinics to girls throughout NYC.

Who is your role model or mentor?
I was lucky to have three high school English teachers who inspired and pushed me to face my own artistic power. This is how we approach the emerging authors of GWN.

What motivates you on a daily basis?
At base, I'm a community organizer. I feel a responsibility to help others realize their desire to have meaningful creative connections. In turn, our community challenges and sustains me.

Kerry Bannigan

Q&A

What are your most popular products or services?
Global Fashion Brands' personal shopping feed as well as the continual discovery of independent brands.

Who is your role model or mentor?
My role model is Richard Branson because his determination, educated risks and courage are an inspiration.

What is your motto or theme song?
Never forget where you come from.

What place inspires you and why?
A family lake house in upstate New York. The silence clears my mind, the scenery inspires me and being by the water relaxes me. A reminder of life outside the city.

GLOBAL FASHION BRANDS

globalfashionbrands.com, Twitter: @missnolcha

Personal. Social. Exclusive.
Global Fashion Brands is a social, online marketplace connecting
savvy shoppers to independent fashion designers and retailers through
a personal shopping and discovery platform. They learn your size,
interests and price range to filter through your favorite stores, brands
and product types to create a truly unique personal shopping feed.

Photos by Belathé Photography

GLOW GLUTEN FREE

800.497.7434
glowglutenfree.com, Twitter: @glowglutenfree

Tasty. Fun. Glowing.
Glow Gluten Free is a NYC allergy-friendly treat company created by a mom with celiac disease. They bake all-natural, wholesome, gluten-free goodies in a dedicated gluten-free kitchen using a secret recipe with a garbanzo bean flour blend in place of traditional wheat flour. Glow Gluten Free cookies can be found in Whole Foods Markets and specialty retailers on the East Coast.

Jill Brack

Q&A

What are your most popular products or services?
We sell four gluten-free cookies: double chocolate, gingersnap, snickerdoodle and, always the best seller, our traditional chocolate chip.

People may be surprised to know...
My husband and I work together 24/7/365 and we're still happily married!

What or who inspired you to start your business?
My remarkable daughter, Stella, has been my inspiration from the start. We really need to name a cookie after her!

What business mistake have you made that you will not repeat?
Kitchen disasters, recipe blunders and cookie carnage were insane before Glow cookies came to be what they are today.

Allison Jagtiani

⬛ Q&A

What are your most popular products or services?
Our top two goji berry cookie flavors are goji cherry cacao and goji ginger walnut.

People may be surprised to know...
Goji berries are considered the "happy berry" because they tend to make you feel good and actually do make people smile! They also happen to be a natural aphrodisiac!

What or who inspired you to start your business?
Goji berries are a very magical berry from the Himalayan mountains that are super-healthy and rich in antioxidants. I wanted to create a company that honored this berry for its super powers and help spread the word to children and adults alike in creating a healthier lifestyle.

GOJI GOURMET

877.EAT.GOJI (328.4654)
gojigourmet.com, Twitter: @GojiGourmet

Delicious. Wholesome. Exotic.
Born in New York City, Goji Gourmet provides goji-licious, guilt-free gourmet snacks. Their goji berry cookies are 100 percent natural, preservative-free and loaded with antioxidant-rich goji berries (eight times more antioxidants than pomegranate!) and other powerful superfoods. Goji Gourmet cookies are low in calories and carbohydrates but satisfying and delicious for any time of the day! Their motto: "For goodness sake, we love goji!"

Soapology photographed by Emily DeWan Photography

What business mistake have you
made that you will not repeat?

*"Thinking I could do it all
by myself. Soliciting help
demonstrates strength and
recognition of the talents
other people can offer."*

Colette Ellis of InStep Consulting

GOTHAM ORGANIZERS

212.866.9493
gothamorganizers.com, Twitter: @GothamOrganizer

Inspiring. Motivating. Life-changing.
For more than 10 years, Gotham Organizers has helped New Yorkers make the most of their space, stuff and time, so they can focus on what's really important in life. They create customized solutions that you can easily maintain and that fit your budget, your style, your life.

Lisa Zaslow

Q&A

What do you like best about owning a business?
The serendipity! I've had opportunities beyond my dreams—being a corporate spokesperson, doing makeover segments on TV, giving talks and workshops that help many people get organized.

Who is your role model or mentor?
My grandmother was a milliner who owned two successful hat and bag shops. As a young girl, she showed me what was possible for women entrepreneurs.

What place inspires you and why?
New York has amazing shops that sell things like marine supplies and restaurant supplies. I get great ideas for storage and organizational solutions for my clients by wandering the streets.

GRAND CRU CLASSES

646.279.8494
GrandCruClasses.com, Twitter: @GrandCruClasses

Fun. Informative. Passionate.
Grand Cru Classes provides fun and informative wine classes and events that unravel
the mysteries of wine. From bachelorette parties and bridal showers to birthdays
and business meetings, Grand Cru Classes can design the perfect wine event
for you. Certified Wine Educator Tracy Ellen Kamens combines her love of wine
with her passion for teaching to craft events that educate as well as entertain.

Tracy Ellen Kamens

 # Q&A

What tip would you give women who are starting a business?
Believe in yourself and follow your dreams even if everyone else thinks you are crazy; you don't want to ever regret what might have been.

Who is your role model or mentor?
My role model is Harriet Lembeck, wine educator and writer, and owner of Harriet Lembeck's Wine & Spirits Program. She embodies the same passion I do and is well respected in our industry.

What is your motto or theme song?
Life's too short to drink bad wine, and everything in moderation... including moderation.

How do you relax?
I relax with a glass of wine, of course.

Tamiko Helen Hargrove

Q&A

What are your most popular
products or services?
Hand-poured, beautifully packaged,
scented soy candles.

People may be surprised to know...
The name Helen Julia was inspired by
my grandmothers, Helen and Julia!

Where is your favorite place to
go with your girlfriends?
Sunday brunch for a nice early-
afternoon girl chat!

How do you spend your free time?
With family. My 2-year-old niece is the
cutest to watch as she explores.

What is your indulgence?
Shopping at my favorite apparel store for
new designs (hopefully during a sale).

HELEN JULIA
NEW YORK

718.619.2267
helenjulia.com, Twitter: @helenjuliainc

Luxury. Classic. Natural.
Helen Julia's aromatic candle scents are based on simple accords of
fragrance notes. Each candle inspires distinct moods, rich in meaning
and memories. Scents include: I Do, Prima Donna, Magnolia Bliss,
Cashmere Cloud, Chocolate Pear-adise and Terrycloth Robe, to name
a few. All of Helen Julia fragrance candles are available in 10.5 oz and
3 oz, along with their individual velvet pouch—perfect for traveling.

Danielle "Miss Journey" Fontus

Q&A

What are your most popular products or services?
Her Journey Girls Night Out! We encourage women to try new things, from new food to flying trapeze. Our friendly environment also allows women to connect with one another.

What tip would you give women who are starting a business?
Surround yourself with others who are in line with your vision. Their wisdom and support can certainly take you further than you may go on your own.

What do you like best about owning a business?
I most enjoy the freedom that comes from making my own decisions. It is also so fulfilling to truly enjoy what I do.

HER JOURNEY

herjourneymag.com, Twitter: @HerJourneyMag

Exciting. Adventurous. Empowering.

Her Journey is dually dedicated to travel and women's empowerment. It is their mission to expand the reader's traveling horizon by sharing glimpses of extraordinary travel experiences while also guiding her on her individual journey to discover and fulfill her life's purpose. The Her Journey Girls social group is on a mission to share the empowered feeling that comes from exploring beyond one's boundaries.

IN GOOD COMPANY WORKPLACES

16 W 23rd St, 4th Floor, New York, 646.810.9195
ingoodcompanyworkplaces.com, Twitter: @ingoodcmpny

Innovative. Energetic. Dynamic.

In Good Company Workplaces is a collaborative work space that gives women entrepreneurs flexible access to part-time and full-time professional space as well as access to colleagues, collaboration and educational programs that help you build your business. Membership is a wonderful asset to women business owners and aspiring business owners. In Good Company's aim is to redefine the way women work for themselves and experience entrepreneurship.

Amy Abrams and Adelaide Lancaster

Q&A

People may be surprised to know...
We have business owners from almost every industry and our members' ages range from 25 to 75! We use our flexible work space the same way our members do!

Who is your role model or mentor?
Adelaide: I have so many people who I love to learn from. Anna Quindlan is one, Terry Gross is another, Jon Stewart is, too. Each have carved out a unique and meaningful role for themselves and made valuable contributions to the social dialogue.

Where is your favorite place to go with your girlfriends?
Amy: For a drink! Although I can never have more than one!
Adelaide: I love tapas places (olives and cheese, yum)!

Chelsea

Colette Ellis

 Q&A

People may be surprised to know...
I've worked in the corporate, nonprofit
and government sectors. The one aspect
they all have in common—people!

What or who inspired you to
start your business?
The changing economy sparked my
desire to create spaces for learning
and discovery that empower leaders
to find their next adventure.

Who is your role model or mentor?
Among others, I'm inspired by my
grandfather for his compassion, work ethic
and avid desire for continuous learning.

What business mistake have you
made that you will not repeat?
Thinking I could do it all by myself. Soliciting
help demonstrates strength and recognition
of the talents other people can offer.

How do you spend your free time?
Exploring different neighborhoods
in New York City; spending time
with family and friends.

Where is your favorite place to
go with your girlfriends?
A fun cafe or wine bar where we can linger,
catch up and indulge in tasty treats!

INSTEP CONSULTING

646.450.4380
instepconsulting.com, Twitter: @coach_colette

Dynamic. Holistic. Visionary.
InStep Consulting is a nationally recognized coaching and consulting company that helps clients leverage their passion, power and relationships to achieve sustainable results. They have been coaching and training Fortune 500 and nonprofit leaders in effective communication since 1998. They show how to lead your team through change. As an InStep client, you can expect an honest, responsive partner who enhances your learning, lifestyle and legacy!

Photos by A. Anaiz Photography, except portrait by Emily DeWan Photography

JAN CONSULTING GROUP, LLP

212.933.4128, ljanicki@janconsultinggroup.com
janconsultinggroup.com, businessconsultingnow.com, Twitter: @businessplanjcg

Creative. Trusted. Knowledgeable.
Jan Consulting Group is a boutique management consulting firm working with entrepreneurs and small-business owners since 1996 and helping them start, grow and sustain their companies. They develop creative business strategies and support business owners in realizing their business vision. They also help clients develop the management, financial and sales infrastructure to support sustainable growth. They are the go-to small-business gurus!

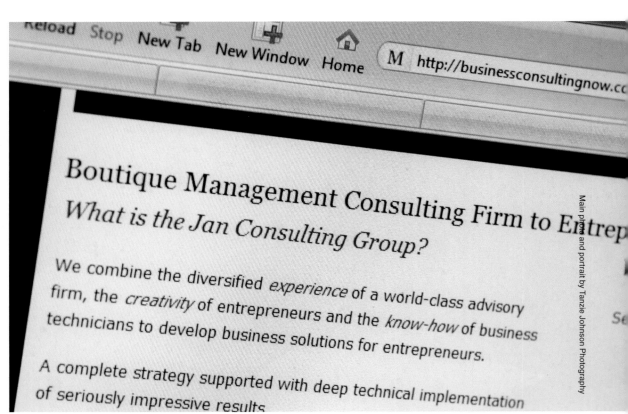

Reload Stop New Tab New Window Home M http://businessconsultingnow.cc

Boutique Management Consulting Firm to Entrep
What is the Jan Consulting Group?

We combine the diversified *experience* of a world-class advisory firm, the *creativity* of entrepreneurs and the *know-how* of business technicians to develop business solutions for entrepreneurs.

A complete strategy supported with deep technical implementation of seriously impressive results

Main photo and portrait by Tanzie Johnson Photography

Lisa Janicki

Q&A

What are your most popular products or services?
Business plans for raising capital, strategic planning for growth, outsourced CFO Services, and structuring strategic alliances.

People may be surprised to know...
We work with any budget and all our solutions are custom-tailored based on the unique client situation.

What business mistake have you made that you will not repeat?
When I became a business owner, I thought my business was consulting and I was only half right. Marketing and sales is the other half of my business.

Where is your favorite place to go with your girlfriends?
Great Jones Spa—their water lounge feels like an urban oasis and mini-vacation.

What or who inspired you to start your business?
My mom. She gave me the courage to break from the norm of my profession at the time and follow my big business ideas.

Who is your role model or mentor?
My mentor on a professional level is my dad, who has been a professional consultant for more than 40 years. My role model as a female entrepreneur is Madonna.

JEN HUANG PHOTOGRAPHY

347.323.5736
jenhuangphotography.com, Twitter: @jenhuangphoto

Fresh. Clean. Romantic.

Jen Huang approaches wedding photography with a romantic, fine-art sensibility. She is known for her fresh, clean, light-filled images and striking portraits. Her passion for photography is exemplified in her continued dedication to medium-format film and the resulting work has appeared in bridal editorials all over the country.

Photos by Jen Huang Photography

Jen Huang

Q&A

What tip would you give women who are starting a business?
Be kind to everyone—it is always appreciated and will make you feel at ease even on the toughest days.

Who is your role model or mentor?
My family is incredible. Their ability to sacrifice, work hard and dedicate themselves to their passions has always inspired me to be the best that I can be.

How do you relax?
I try to travel as often as possible, I'd like to eventually see the whole world!

What do you CRAVE?
Well-crafted objects, for example, an old Hermes typewriter, a wrought iron French campaign bed, a railroad tie dining table, and film cameras they don't make anymore!

Jillian Wright

 # Q&A

Who is your role model or mentor?
Dawn Gantt from Bioelements. Her wealth of aesthetic knowledge is awe-inspiring. My secret role model is Erica Gragg, who founded Escape to Shape. She combines travel, fitness, culture and spa services, and brings her guests to unique locations all over the world. She's my hero!

What business mistake have you made that you will not repeat?
Bigger isn't always better. A smaller, more controlled environment allows for better service, more creativity, superior therapists and refined hospitality.

What is your indulgence?
My favorite indulgences are dinner parties with my close friends and seeing my young children discover new things in life.

JILLIAN WRIGHT
CLINICAL SKIN SPA

JILLIAN WRIGHT
CLINICAL SKIN SPA

22 E 66th St, 2nd Floor, New York, 212.249.2230
jillianwrightclinicalskinspa.com, Twitter: @jwclinicalskin

Innovative. Results-oriented. Down-home.
Over the last decade, Jillian Wright based her aesthetic practice on
a trinity combining her heart, mind and hands. Jillian believes that
successful skin-care practices need this recipe to deliver superior facial
and massage treatments. Jillian and her staff offer an array of skin
and body therapies that are corrective yet pampering in nature.

Jo Laurie

Q&A

What are your most popular products or services?
Custom furniture and artisan-inspired millwork. Complete concept origination including design development and implementation. Hospitality/commercial. Delivery of wholly unique spaces.

Who is your role model or mentor?
Coco Chanel, who was truly light years ahead of her time in many ways, especially in design and in business. Plus, my grandmother, who said, "Do it... because your generation can!"

What do you CRAVE?
Opportunities for all women globally, starting with reproductive choices. Clients interested in working with us to push design parameters. Health, happiness and more travel!

JO LAURIE DESIGN

212.460.9299
jolauriedesign.com, Twitter: @jolauriedesign

Innovative. Unadulterated. Cosmopolitan.
Jo Laurie Design, a multidisciplinary architectural interior design and branding company, has been operating from downtown Manhattan for more than 15 years. Projects range from high-end residential renovations to hospitality and commercial. Turning your vision into reality—within your budget and time frame—is their specialty, and they provide everything from architects to websites. JLD has an extensive portfolio of international award-winning projects.

Portrait, main and upper middle photos by A. Anaiz Photography, upper left and right photos by Jo Laurie Design

JOAN HORNIG
PHILANTHROPY IS BEAUTIFUL®

212.427.6216
joanhornig.com

Philanthropic. Empowering. Effective.
Joan Hornig Philanthropy is Beautiful® is designed to make a statement—and a difference. Merging women's passions for jewelry and giving back, the company's unique model leverages the "power of the purse." With 100% of the profit on every sale donated to the charity of the purchaser's choice, women are empowered to use beauty and fashion for the benefit of others. Support has been provided to hundreds of nonprofits throughout the US and abroad. Launched by Bergdorf Goodman and found through other fine retailers across the country.

Joan Hornig

 # Q&A

What tip would you give women who are starting a business?
Believe in yourself and your power to realize your vision. Work with young, passionate and talented people. Be scrappy and utilize all the advantages and cost savings provided by technology.

What do you like best about owning a business?
Freedom to set standards and direction of the business. Working with people I respect and enjoy. Realizing my dream of giving away all of the profits to charity.

Who is your role model or mentor?
In addition to my family, Paul Newman who pointed the way to combine consumer products with philanthropy and Oprah who illustrates that a woman can move mountains regardless of modest beginnings.

JOULEBODY

917.612.5827
joulebody.com, Twitter: @joulebody

Energetic. Fresh. Organic.
Joulebody is a lifestyle management program designed for new beginnings
in health and weight. Joulebody's programs are for urban warriors juggling
professional and home life on a daily basis and who therefore can't find time for
personal wellness. Joulebody has grown by adding an additional service/product,
The Kickstart Diet, which is a vegan, food-cleansing meal replacement program
that can be a short commitment starting from three days up to 21 days.

Photos by Emily DeWan Photography

Yvette Rose

Q&A

What do you like best about owning a business?
I get to do what I really love instead of doing what I have to do to get a paycheck. I come to work every day because I want to.

Who is your role model or mentor?
My husband is my role model. He keeps his cool. He is there for anyone who needs him. He is honest and believes in hard work.

How do you relax?
I relax by listening to music and drinking wine while cooking food. I love that combo. Even if it's only for me.

What place inspires you and why?
The place that most inspires me is Coney Island. I never want to go back, yet I know it is the place that helped mold me into who I am.

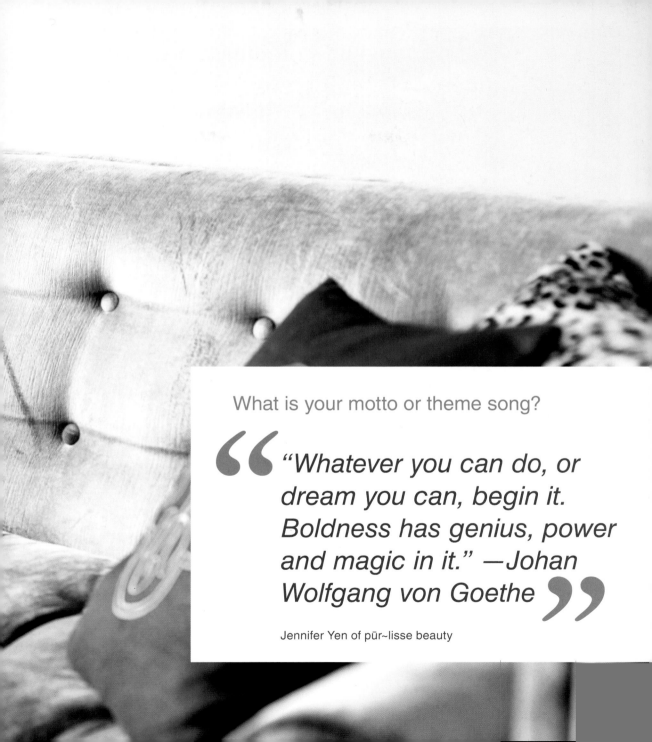

What is your motto or theme song?

" *"Whatever you can do, or dream you can, begin it. Boldness has genius, power and magic in it."* —*Johan Wolfgang von Goethe* "

Jennifer Yen of pūr~lisse beauty

Photos by Kat Thek, except portrait by Scott Jones

JOURNELLE

3 E 17th St, New York, 212.255.7802
125 Mercer St, New York, 212.255.7803
journelle.com, Twitter: @clairejournelle, Twitter: @shopjournelle

Elegant. Warm. Zen.

Journelle is a lingerie concept for modern women, with two stores in New York City and a third in Miami Beach. Taking inspiration from the archaic French word *journellement*, which means "daily," owner Claire Chambers and the Journelle team provide a tastefully curated selection of lingerie from top brands, expert assistance and a beautiful environment.

Claire Chambers

 # Q&A

What are your most popular products or services?
Lingerie from top brands such as Chantelle, Elle Macpherson Intimates, Hanky Panky, Eberjey, La Perla and many more.

What do you like best about owning a business?
Choosing the team of people I get to work with.

What motivates you on a daily basis?
Seeing the company grow and helping women feel great about themselves.

What place inspires you and why?
Strangely, I'm always inspired on airplanes. I'm up in the air, no one can reach me and I suddenly think of all these ideas!

What do you CRAVE?
Happiness.

SoHo

Flatiron

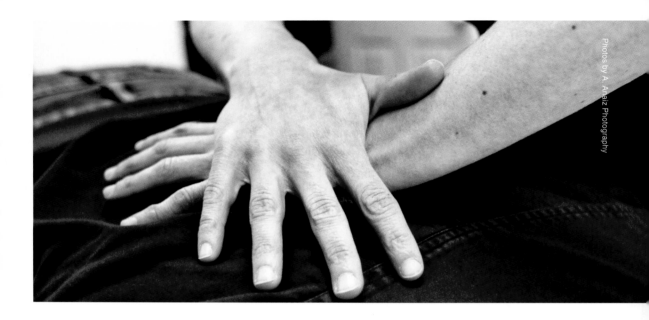

KAREN LITZY, MSPT
PHYSICAL THERAPIST

347.565.5578
karenlitzy.com, Twitter: @karenlitzynyc

HEALTHY WEALTHY &
SMART RADIO SHOW

talkingalternative.com

Holistic. Hands-on. Compassionate.
Karen Litzy is a licensed physical therapist who specializes in private home/
office—based PT. She knows that New Yorkers have busy schedules and strives
to make PT more convenient by coming to them. Her hands-on approach to
patient care, along with careful exercise prescription, has resulted in outstanding
results for her patients. She treats the person, not just the diagnosis.

Karen Litzy,
MSPT

 # Q&A

What do you like best about owning a business?
I love being able to take my ideas and turn them into real results of which I can be proud. I also love the freedom of setting my own schedule!

What motivates you on a daily basis?
My patients. Knowing that I can make a positive difference not only in their health but in their overall lives is a very powerful motivator.

What place inspires you and why?
My monthly women's entrepreneurial group meeting. I always leave feeling positive and motivated to push forward with my ideas and they give me the confidence to execute them!

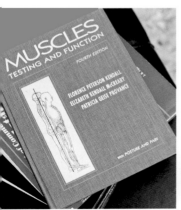

Katrina Kelly

Q&A

What are your most popular products or services?
My 7 Layers of Love® charms, rings and KK logo drop charms.

What tip would you give women who are starting a business?
Start a business with a product or service that you genuinely respect, admire and love.

What motivates you on a daily basis?
Knowing that women shine from the inside and out when they don jewels.

What is your motto or theme song?
Love the life you live and live the life you love.

What place inspires you and why?
Wherever I am inspires me. To me, inspiration is a state of mind that I create.

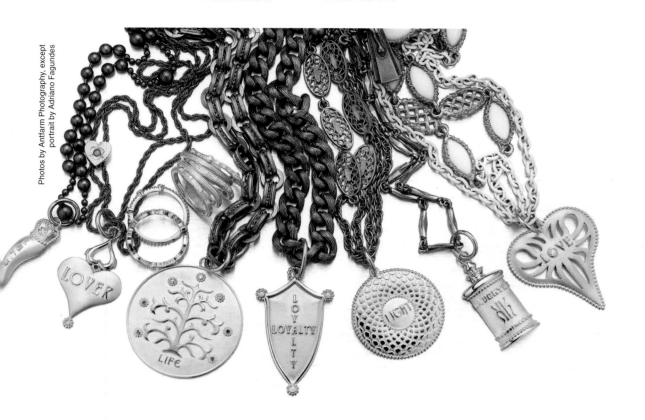

Photos by Antfarm Photography, except portrait by Adriano Fagundes

KATRINA KELLY JEWELRY

917.331.8619
katrinakellyjewelry.com, Twitter: @katrinakelly

Beautiful. Empowering. Enduring.
Katrina Kelly Jewelry is an heirloom-influenced collection that fuses cultures and combines fine intricate design with an old-world feel. The launch of her 7 Layers of Love® Collection took the company to another level and became a top seller for brides. Each piece is a timeless expression of the wearer's deepest feelings and most heartfelt sentiments.

Laura
Geller

Q&A

What tip would you give women who are starting a business?

It isn't going to be a gravy train, especially at the beginning; you may have to work for less knowing that the future you're working toward holds something bigger.

What do you like best about owning a business?

I am blazing my own trail and following my personal vision. I surround myself with experts in all fields to help me on my journey toward success.

What do you CRAVE?

Chocolate on a regular basis, and Italian food! Above all I crave the one-on-one time spent unwinding with my son—it both grounds me and recharges me at once!

LAURA GELLER MAKEUP

1044 Lexington Ave, New York, 212.570.5477
laurageller.com, Twitter: @laurageller

Ingenious. Fun. Timeless.

In 1993, Laura opened Laura Geller Makeup Studios on New York City's Upper East Side. The purpose was to teach women the how-to of cosmetics. Her hands-on, multitasking approach has allowed her to demystify makeup for all women. She provides tools needed to create both basic and breathtaking looks. The studio has become a "living laboratory" and showcase for her eponymous line of cosmetics.

Tanya Brown

Q&A

What are your most popular products or services?
The Sexy Seductress has been a winner right out of the gate. Followed by the Moonstone Choker.

Who is your role model or mentor?
My grandmother. She has been an incredibly supportive person who has guided me all my life. Lauren St. Julian is dedicated to her—an amazing woman.

How do you relax?
Give me a great book or foreign film and I can zone out. On a bad day, a musical lifts my spirits and gives me my second wind.

LAUREN ST. JULIAN

By appointment only: 108 14th St, Ste 1 A, Hoboken
laurenstjulian.com, single-bliss.com, Twitter: @Singledashbliss

Beautiful. Stunning. Classic.
Tanya Brown found that the styles in the stores all looked the same so she
started designing pieces that she wanted to wear. From chunky cocktail rings
to beautiful necklaces that look fabulous with a white button-down shirt and
jeans as well as rock (no pun intended) a little black dress. At first filling a void
for pieces that Tanya could not find, the collection has evolved into a beautiful
line that others covet as well. Tanya achieves her goals while honoring her
grandmother, who is aptly named Lauren St. Julian, in creating the line she loves.

LIZ LANGE MATERNITY

Located at Target stores nationwide
lizlange.com

COMPLETELY ME
BY LIZ LANGE

fashion.hsn.com

SHOPAFROLIC.COM

shopafrolic.com, Twitter: @Shopafrolic

Innovative. Trend-setting. Sophisticated.

In 1997, Liz Lange created Liz Lange Maternity, changing forever the face of maternity fashions. In 2007, after dressing every major pregnant celebrity, forging licensing deals with Nike and Target (Liz Lange for Target is the exclusive maternity department at all Target locations), Lange sold her business though she continues on as the face of the brand. Last year her non-maternity clothing collection, Completely Me by Liz Lange, debuted on HSN, and she co-founded the popular woman's shopping site, Shopafrolic.com.

Liz Lange

Q&A

What tip would you give women who are starting a business?
You almost have to cover your ears to shut out all the negativity and naysayers. Believe in yourself no matter what, because it's hard to be an entrepreneur.

What is your favorite part about owning a small business?
I feel so lucky to love what I do. I work *very* hard, I'm very invested emotionally and I really care about my work. And, as a mother, I feel so fortunate that my job allows flexibility.

Who is your role model or mentor?
There are so many women who I look up to. Mary Wells Lawrence, an important figure in advertising, is a great example, as is Estée Lauder. There are a few well-known businessmen who motivate me: Phil Knight, Howard Schultz and Tony Hsieh.

LUXURYMONOGRAMS.COM

LuxuryMonograms.com, Melanie@LuxuryMonograms.com

Playful. Sophisticated. Personalized.
Luxury Monograms is an online store that allows you to create customized contemporary home decor items and bags. You select your product, fabric and monogram style to create the ultimate personalized piece! Choose from throw pillows, place mats and bags made from fabrics such as boldly colored chevrons, ikats, animal prints, stripes and florals. These are monogrammed pieces for a new generation.

Melanie
Duncan

 # Q&A

What are your most popular products or services?
Our custom throw pillows and bags are very popular. However, brides love our place mats and napkins in their new homes.

What tip would you give women who are starting a business?
Pace yourself. Start small and get your idea out there so that you can invest in your business as you grow, instead of getting in over your head.

What is your motto or theme song?
"Life isn't about finding yourself. Life is about creating yourself." —George Bernard Shaw

What place inspires you and why?
New York City—because every person and place has such an incredible story, and by living here you get to become a part of it.

Kalliopi and Artemis Kohas

 # Q&A

What are your most popular products or services?
Mastiha was the first natural chewing gum, so our gums are the most popular. They prevent plaque and gingivitis!

People may be surprised to know...
Chios Mastiha kills H. pylori bacteria and combats acid reflux, ulcers and Crohn's disease.

What or who inspired you to start your business?
We were inspired by our deep love for our roots and heritage. Chios Mastiha has an amazing history and the shops are a brilliant way of modernizing this ancient super-resin while telling its story. Having grown up with Mastiha, our parents having cultivated it themselves, we wanted to be a part of it!

MASTIHASHOP

145 Orchard St, New York, 212.253.0895
mastihashopny.com, Twitter: @mastihashopny, info@mastihashopny.com

Natural. Healthy. Unique.

mastihashop NY is the first retail outpost of the official shops of the Chios
Mastiha Growers Association. They feature natural products from the eastern
Mediterranean, most with Chios Mastiha—an antibacterial, antioxidant, anti-
inflammatory resin with more than 300 known uses. A fair-trade business
based on an ancient renewable sustainable resource, mastihashop aims
to unite people in their quest for healthy lifestyles and well-being.

 # Q&A

Jacqueline Weppner

What are your most popular products or services?
We help brides in styling all aspects of their wedding day: from finding "the" dress and all the right accessories to developing chic décor details that will have friends and family swooning.

What or who inspired you to start your business?
Shortly after my own New York wedding, I began thinking about what it means to be a city bride. I had searched for an unbiased, style-minded resource. When my search came up short, I set out to create one.

What place inspires you and why?
Paris. The art, the culture, the lifestyle of its people... Parisians live to enjoy life and take such pleasure in little, special details. I find that wonderfully inspiring.

MERCI NEW YORK

60 W 75th St, Ste 5F, New York
mercinewyork.com, Twitter: @MerciNYC

Chic. Stylish. Citified.

Merci New York is a Manhattan-based boutique fashion and event styling service that infuses fêtes, photo shoots, soirees and special occasions with chic details worthy of a magazine tear sheet. While they've been the style-minds behind beauty industry pop-up shops and high-fashion photo shoots, Merci New York also focuses on providing "chic and stylish inspiration for the busy city bride™"—unique services that channel their experiences in the fashion industry and translate them into a high-style NYC bride's big day.

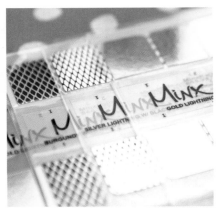

Danielle Corbin Jaime
and Ajanee Alston

Q&A

What are your most popular products or services?
Our most popular services are Bio Sculpture Gel manicures, Minx nail services and Deborah Lippmann Polish.

What do you like best about owning a business?
Interacting with clients is amazing! By the end of each service, we feel like we've made a new friend.

Who is your role model or mentor?
Danielle: Ajanee's constant encouragement is why we started this business together. Also, my husband, Michael, and family and friends who constantly reminded us, "This is your passion; do it."

What do you CRAVE?
Happiness, a thriving business and love from family and friends.

NAIL TAXI NYC

516.476.1696
nailtaxinyc.com, Twitter: @nailtaxinyc

Therapeutic. Tranquil. Pampering.

Nail Taxi NYC is a mobile nail boutique catering to the client who believes that spa services are a necessity, not a luxury. Clients can incorporate spa services into their busy schedules and celebrations. A relaxing spa manicure and pedicure relieves stress, relaxes tense muscles and offers the opportunity to temporarily escape the chaos of multitasking day-to-day routines.

Photos by E. Leigh Photography

NEWLYWISH

212.348.6115
NewlyWish.com, Twitter: @NewlyWish

Innovative. Personalized. Convenient.
NewlyWish is the cure to the common wedding registry. They offer a collection of unique stores and stylish brands, plus a range of nontraditional and experience gift options, allowing engaged couples to create gift registries that truly reflect their personal styles. Plus, they have wonderful ideas for wedding party gifts and favors, so you can share the love with all of your family and friends.

Main photo by Amanda Buzard, portrait by Sofia Negron Photography, upper right pic to by Karen Wise

Amanda Allen

Q&A

What are your most popular products or services?
Kitchen and dinnerware are the most common gifts couples include in their registries; however, many also include experience gifts, with cooking classes and dancing lessons the most popular.

What do you like best about owning a business?
The personal connection and commitment to customers and sense of accomplishment when things go right. Ultimately, you are responsible for the success of your company and the livelihoods of employees.

What motivates you on a daily basis?
Obviously, the overall success of the company, but also keeping an eye on near-term goals and taking things one step at a time. Small accomplishments add up to larger ones!

THE NIC STUDIO

646.470.1642
thenicstudio.com, Twitter: @nicstudio

Stylish. Elegant. Quirky.

The Nic Studio specializes in stationery and prints, characterized by signature illustrations from Nicole Block. With three branches under one roof—NicEvents for custom stationery, NicNotes for notecards or ready-to-order invitations, and NicIllustration for prints and custom artwork—The Nic Studio has you covered. Custom corporate design also available.

Nicole
Block

 # Q&A

What are your most popular products or services?
Custom wedding invitations, ready-to-order bridal collection, private commissioned artwork, and corporate invitations and identity design.

Who is your role model or mentor?
I don't have just one. I have met and continue to meet so many women in the same boat as me. They always inspire me and propel me forward.

What is your motto or theme song?
Just keep swimming.

What do you CRAVE?
Art. Chocolate. Wine. A great dinner out with my husband. A hug and kiss from my daughter. Praise from my mom. And good friends and clients to keep me going.

How do you relax?

We would love to say "a good book" or "a day at the spa" but let's be honest, we relax with a glass of wine and trashy TV!

Dawn Van Dyke and Melina Dreyfuss of DM Events

NYC FACES

868 Metropolitan Ave 2B, Brooklyn, 212.203.5277
nycfaces.net, Twitter: @nycfaces

Approachable. Luxurious. Attentive.
Anni Bruno founded NYC Faces in 2005. She is an on-location, fully
freelance makeup artist. She specializes in bridal work but has experience
designing makeup for all occasions, such as design for theater and film,
and fashion work. Her home base is her studio in Williamsburg, Brooklyn
(aka "The Makeup Loft"), but she is available to travel worldwide.

Anni
Bruno

Q&A

What are your most popular products or services?
Airbrush makeup and individual false eyelashes—they're gorgeous and natural looking.

What tip would you give women who are starting a business?
Learn the art of self-promotion! Don't hesitate to really put yourself out there and meet as many people as you can in your field. Doors will open!

What motivates you on a daily basis?
Knowing that every day I'm connecting with people, making them feel good about themselves and improving their confidence.

What is your motto or theme song?
Motto: "Committed to the Art of Pretty."

Sotiria Krikelis

 # Q&A

What are your most popular products or services?
Our debut product is called Relax Missy; it's the ultimate foldable ballet flat. The designer followers can now wear their sky-high heels and have foldable flats on hand to go from blisters to bliss.

Who is your role model or mentor?
All women who strive for something better in life and have the ambition to make it happen.

Where is your favorite place to go with your girlfriends?
Where else but fabulous Las Vegas! There isn't any other place like it.

ONE LIFE, LIVE-IT, INC.

relaxmissy.com, Twitter: @RelaxMissy

Trendy. Sophisticated. Innovative.

One Life, Live-It, Inc., is a fashion and accessory-minded solutions company catering to the "fashionista frustrations" that plague today's style-conscious woman. Taking its first, fashionable step, Relax Missy foldable ballet flats provide double-duty fashion for stiletto-loving missys. They're sure to be the ultimate wardrobe staple. Comfy couture never looked so good!

Juli Oliver

Q&A

People may be surprised to know...
I work really well under stress or in a
time crunch. I never stop multitasking.

What or who inspired you to
start your business?
First and foremost my creativity,
but also working with large families
in the past with a lot of household
possessions gave way to my obsession
with "ridding the world of clutter."

Who is your role model or mentor?
Having passed on their hard-working,
never-slow-down business nature to me,
my parents are my role models. No matter
where I choose to go or what I choose to
do, I always have their love and support.

What is your indulgence?
Cheese, chocolate, and being
outdoors in the sun!

ORGANIZENY

315.559.4845
organizeny.com, Twitter: @OrganizeNY

Essential. Creative. Efficient.
Working with families, small businesses and home offices, owner Juli Oliver solves
organizing dilemmas from Washington Heights to Beijing, all while maintaining
a loyal NYC customer base. OrganizeNY offers assistance to clients who need
help with household clutter, paper management, relocation, and countless other
personal-assistant services to achieve balance, success and peace of mind!

Photos by Missy Photography

PAWFECT DAY

16 W 23rd St, 4th Floor, New York, 917.456.0330
pawfectday.com, Twitter: @PawfectDay

Personal. Reliable. Professional.
Bonded and insured, Pawfect Day tailors to you and your pet's needs with high-quality attention to detail. As pet owners themselves, they know the importance of finding a trusted pet caregiver. They believe that pets are family and should be treated accordingly. When initiating services with Pawfect Day, you become part of their family. Contact them for a complimentary consultation and mention CRAVE for a discount.

Jacqueline Rivera

Q&A

People may be surprised to know...
My first rescue was a chicken. As a child, I found a dirty, rain-soaked chicken on the streets of Washington Heights and brought him home. In spite of coming home to a pearly white chicken in a fish tank, my mother was not too pleased.

Who is your role model or mentor?
Judy Josey. She mentored me as a freshman in college and has always believed in me. She is truly an inspiration and has taught me strength and perseverance. We have kept in touch ever since and she is my second mom.

How do you spend your free time?
Going to animal rescue socials, fundraising walks and riding my bike by the East River.

What is your indulgence?
Smoothies—can't get enough of them. My personal favorite is strawberry, banana and pineapple with coconut flakes!

What do you CRAVE? In business? In life?
I crave finding daily fulfillment in all I do in the midst of the daily hustle and bustle of NYC.

Flatiron

Q&A

Who is your role model or mentor?
All the other small business owners making things happen for themselves and their businesses and, of course, my mother who taught me how to stitch!

What motivates you on a daily basis?
The opportunity that starting this business has afforded me to inspire people to be creative, try something new and feel good about something they have made.

What is your motto or theme song?
"We do not remember days, we remember the moments." —Cesare Pavese

How do you relax?
Going for walks with my puppy, Molly, taking yoga, reading and exploring all the fun and interesting design and creative-driven websites and blogs out there.

Rachel Low

PINS & NEEDLES

1045 Lexington Ave, 2nd Floor, New York, 212.535.6222
pinsandneedlesnyc.com, Twitter: @startstitching.com

Handmade. Modern. Inspiring.
Pins & Needles (P&N) is a sewing, fabric crafts and needlework shop located
on the Upper East Side of NYC. This gem of a store offers everything from
fun and unique fabric for fashion, home decor and craft sewing to fabulous
painted needlepoint canvases and supplies. What's more, P&N offers private
and group lessons, classes and workshops on all kinds of stitching.

Photos by A. Anaiz Photography

POPPIES & POSIES
FLORAL AND EVENT DESIGN

By appointment only: 153 Roebling St, Ste 4E, Brooklyn, 347.709.0762
poppiesandposiesevents.com, poppiesandposiesevents.blogspot.com, Twitter: @poppiesposies

Stylish. Unique. Vibrant.
Poppies & Posies is a boutique floral and event design firm based in New York City. Every detail of their fabulous fetes are meticulously designed and, whenever possible, handcrafted. Their arrangements are inspired by the organic movement and composition of the country gardens that both girls spent sunny summer days in as children. They love what they do and hope you will too!

Juliet Totten and Sierra Yaun

 # Q&A

What or who inspired you to start your business?
Our families both inspired us to start our business. Sierra's mother is a successful small-business owner and Juliet's father was an avid gardener. They've both influenced our lives greatly.

Who is your role model or mentor?
Jacqueline Kennedy. Her style is timeless.

How do you spend your free time?
We try to take advantage of this fabulous city we live in. There are countless parks, cafés, museums and restaurants to keep us busy. We adore this new Upper West Side restaurant, Recipe, and keep going back for their delicious cocktails and rustic chic atmosphere.

Melissa Wildstein,
Katie Hellmuth Martin
and Sabina Ptacin

Q&A

**What tip would you give women
who are starting a business?**
Get tapped into a supportive community of
like-minded people, prepare yourself to wear
a lot of hats and learn when to delegate.

**What do you like best about owning
a business?**
Freedom to adapt and create as
needed. The way it pushes you beyond
what you thought you were capable
of. The creative results and lessons
we get from a good challenge.

What motivates you on a daily basis?
Creating things. Our amazing team. The
possibility of magnificent developments!

What do you CRAVE?
Happiness, inner peace and good
coffee. Others to feel the buzz
entrepreneurship brings!

'PRENEUR

preneur.net, Twitter: @preneuring

Forward-thinking. Strong. Collaborative.

'PRENEUR showcases and offers educational resources and a community for entrepreneurs. Whether in person or online, 'PRENEUR is your connection to others you can turn to for advice, education, collaborations, referrals, partnerships and even the occasional commiseration. The 'PRENEUR team and community is full of constant connectors, creators of "aha" moments, cheerleaders whether you're up or down, and supporters who empower you daily via membership tools and benefits.

Main photo by Doug Ross, portrait and lower left and middle photos by Annelize Bester I THUTO

PŪR~LISSE BEAUTY

310.430.8989
purlisse.com, Twitter: @purlisse

Beautiful. Graceful. Scientific.

pūr~lisse is a cosmeceutical solution for sensitive skin and age prevention inspired by Jennifer Yen's grandmother's Chinese beauty wisdom and advanced skin science. pūr~lisse's scientifically proven ingredients make up the Lotus Lupine 5 Complex (blue lotus, white tea, lupine peptides, sea silk, soy protein), which offers superior anti-aging properties. All pūr~lisse products are free of parabens, petrochemicals, phathalates and animal by-products, synthetic colors and fragrance.

 # Q&A

Jennifer Yen

What tip would you give women who are starting a business?
Have passion and love what you do. This is the only way you will have the energy and stamina for the challenges and unexpected obstacles of starting a new business.

What do you like best about owning a business?
Doing what I love and creating amazing skincare products for people.

Who is your role model or mentor?
Women like Madame C. J. Walker, Hillary Clinton, Cristina Carlino and my mother. All of them are strong, smart, wise, driven and have defied the odds.

What is your motto or theme song?
"Whatever you can do, or dream you can, begin it. Boldness has genius, power and magic in it." —Johan Wolfgang von Goethe

Elizabeth Stein

Q&A

What are your most popular products or services?
Chocolate chip cookie mix.

What or who inspired you to start your business?
I was fed up with all the unhealthy baking choices on the market and wanted to provide a nutritious, tasty alternative.

Who is your role model or mentor?
All the other small, young, conscious companies who are helping to make a difference in the healthy food movement.

What is your indulgence?
Traveling, eating at farm-to-table restaurants and sleeping in.

PURELY ELIZABETH

646.330.5825
purelyelizabeth.com, Twitter: @purelyelizabeth

Pure. Healthy. Real.
Purely elizabeth makes delicious gourmet baking mixes, using the highest-quality natural and organic ingredients, loaded with health benefits and free of the bad stuff (sugar, dairy, wheat or gluten). Just pure and honest. Good for you and the planet!

Bryn Taylor

What are your most popular products or services?
Closet cleaning and wardrobe revamping for women over 40—both one-on-one and through helpful online tips.

What do you like best about owning a business?
I have to answer to myself at the end of the day, which makes me work the hardest but also reaps the most satisfaction.

Who is your role model or mentor?
My smart and stylish mother who's incredibly candid about the issues she's faced after 40. She is the inspiration behind The Re-Stylist.

What do you CRAVE?
I crave helping women feel confident through a simple change of clothes. It can do wonders!

THE RE-STYLIST

therestylist.com, 973.979.4771, Twitter: @TheReStylist

Chic. Creative. Empowering.
The Re-Stylist is a personal styling service and website devoted entirely to the fashion needs of women over 40. The Re-Stylist offers unique, practical advice either face-to-face with professional stylist, Bryn Taylor, or via the web with helpful tips on everything from how to find the right pair of jeans to what shoes to wear to your daughter's wedding.

Amy W. Shapiro MS, RD, CDN

Q&A

What are your most popular products or services?
One-on-one nutrition counseling, supermarket tours and pantry/kitchen makeovers.

People may be surprised to know...
I eat chocolate every day!

What or who inspired you to start your business?
My family and my previous experiences working for other companies. I have tons of ideas, now I can execute them.

Who is your role model or mentor?
My sister, who has been a successful business owner for over five years and my best friend for over 30!

What is your indulgence?
Chocolate, wine and shopping!

REAL NUTRITION NYC

16 W 23rd St, 4th Floor, New York, 646.269.8205
realnutritionnyc.com, Twitter: @RealNutritionNY

Realistic. Supportive. Effective.
Real Nutrition NYC solves the nutritional challenges served up by everyday life. Whether you want to lose weight, treat a medical condition, boost your physical performance and fitness levels, or learn how to make healthier food choices, they will help you meet and maintain your individual goals through realistic solutions designed for your lifestyle. Lively and interactive corporate wellness and media events are also scheduled regularly.
Real Nutrition NYC's motto: "Real food. Real life. Real solutions."

Photos by A. Green

Chelsea

REBECCA LUKE STYLE

646.688.5846
rebeccalukestyleblog.com, Twitter: @rebeccaluke

LES EGOISTES
CREATIVE SERVICES

646.688.5846
lesegoistes.com

Relevant. Stylish. Perceptive.

Rebecca Luke founded les Egoistes in 2000 and Rebecca Luke Style in 2008. Les Egoistes focuses their creative services on anything requiring an image. A stylist, costume designer and personal image consultant, Rebecca speaks internationally on sustainable fashion and building a wardrobe. She is a published author and blogs about fashion and lifestyle.

Rebecca Luke

 # Q&A

What are your most popular
products or services?
Personal styling and closet consultations.

What tip would you give women
who are starting a business?
Do your research and be willing to be
flexible as you develop your concepts.

Who is your role model or mentor?
Coco Chanel.

What is your biggest fear?
Ill-fitting clothing.

What is your motto or theme song?
"It's better to be looked over than
overlooked."—Mae West

What place inspires you and why?
Paris, for the sheer chicness of it
all and New York, for its people.

Pins & Needles photographed
by A. Anaiz Photography

What tip would you give women who are starting a business?

" Be kind to everyone—it is always appreciated and will make you feel at ease even on the toughest days. "

Jen Huang of Jen Huang Photography

ROCK PAPER SCISSORS EVENTS

212.675.2202
rpscissors.com, Twitter: @rpsevents

Creative. Flexible. Affordable.

Rock Paper Scissors Events is a new boutique event design firm. Their designs have already captivated and inspired the industry and clients, quickly earning them a place among the most stylish in the business. Think of them as interior designers for your events. Blog darlings, specializing in weddings, social events and branding events like launch parties, they even offer flexible and affordable hourly pricing.

Ara Farnam

Q&A

What are your most popular products or services?
Most clients love our flexible hourly consulting that allows them to choose how much or how little help they need, along with a day-of setup package.

What place inspires you and why?
Having my background in interior design, I go back to my interior design magazine collection. Those have been, and probably always will be, my go-to for a shot of inspiration.

What do you CRAVE?
I crave being deliciously in love, with beautiful surroundings, gorgeous flowers, inspiring patterns, unexpected color choices, fantastic hotels with even more fantastic service, a good laugh and some fun adventure.

Rebecca Rodskog

▪️ Q&A

What tip would you give women who are starting a business?
Start small and build on success. Don't let yourself get overwhelmed with the prospects of what's next—focus on actions and momentum. And ask for help!

What do you like best about owning a business?
The flexibility of choosing where I want to grow my business. I am grateful to have full control over who I choose to work with and when.

Who is your role model or mentor?
Seth Godin. His motto of "go do something!" is my MO. I believe in taking action, even if it means failing.

What motivates you on a daily basis?
A deep desire to help people. Whenever overwhelmed, I step back and say: "What's the one thing I can do today that will help someone?" And then I do it.

What is your motto or theme song?
"Life is to be lived. If you have to support yourself, you had bloody well better find some way that is going to be interesting." —Katharine Hepburn

RODSKOG CHANGE CONSULTING

415.235.3213
rodskog.com, Twitter: @beccalynn

Inspiring. Engaging. Connected.
Rodskog Change Consulting supports entrepreneurial-spirited women
in the pursuit of making their dreams a reality. With more than 18 years'
experience in change management, Rebecca has deep insight into what
breeds successful changes in one's life—both personally and professionally.
Rebecca's ability to deeply understand each individual's journey and help
guide them toward their vision of success is the foundation of her practice.

Photos by Iris Bachman

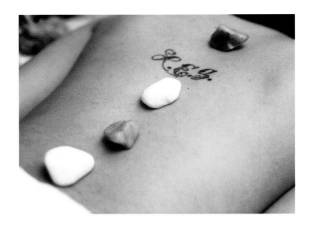

Christine Gutierrez

Q&A

What are your most popular products or services?
IntenSession healing and massage and intuitive counseling/life coaching.

What tip would you give women who are starting a business?
Listen to your intuition, she whispers to you.

What do you like best about owning a business?
Being able to do what I love daily—inspiring women all over the world to be their best selves and spreading this message of love.

Who is your role model or mentor?
Terri Cole, Kris Carr, Bianca Beldini, Gabrielle Bernstein, Sera Beak, my mom and dad and all those who live from the heart.

What motivates you on a daily basis?
Being connected to the endless supply of love energy around me, and the beautiful women I work with.

What is your motto or theme song?
"Ignite Spirit. Expand Consciousness."

What place inspires you and why?
Puerto Rico, the land of my cultural roots. I feel the warmth of the people and love the food and nature. The colors are vibrant and I feel alive when there.

SACRED SPACE NYC

By appointment only: 280 Madison Ave, New York, 646.240.6747
sacredspacenyc.org, Twitter: @sacredspacenyc

Innovative. Spirited. Holistic.
Sacred Space NYC (SSNYC) is a women's wellness company that offers tailored,
spirited relaxation and wellness treatments, including massage, healing, life coaching
and holistic health coaching. Offering an oasis from the hectic urban life in one of
their relaxing NYC studios, SSNYC offers the chance for a rejuvenating experience.
Featured in *Time Out NY* magazine, the intenSession method fuses intention-setting,
guided breath-work, meditation, reiki and positive affirmations. Sacred Space NYC
has reinvented the world of relaxation: come and ignite your inner goddess!

Photos by Belathée Photography

Murray Hill

Sadia Seymour

 # Q&A

What are your most popular products or services?
The Closet Clean Out helps women revamp or update their existing wardrobe. The Personal Shopping package helps you expand your wardrobe while having an expert by your side.

What do you like best about owning a business?
I love the freedom to be able to do what I love and still have the option to have a full personal life. The key is time management.

Who is your role model or mentor?
My mother is my role model. She is not in the industry, but she led by example that you can have whatever you want, if you work hard for it.

What place inspires you and why?
New York City! Do you really need to ask?

SADIA SEYMOUR FASHION STYLIST

516.356.6188
sadiaseymour.com

Stylish. Friendly. Creative.

New York–native fashion stylist Sadia Seymour loves everything fashion! She has been a professional stylist for over 10 years and loves to work with women in addition to styling for catalogs, editorial, print ads and commercials. Sadia's knowledge of the fashion industry and expertise on where to shop for all budgets make shopping with her a truly satisfying experience. There's a package for everyone!

Erin L. Schiffman

Q&A

What are your most popular products or services?
Logo and brand identity, packaging, marketing collateral and websites.

People may be surprised to know...
We started our business with a small amount of money from our savings and zero clients. Scary!

What or who inspired you to start your business?
The lack of passion and creativity from my previous jobs was a huge motivator as well as my entrepreneurial family.

Who is your role model or mentor?
Dolly Parton—she is a true rags-to-riches story. She has a shrewd business sense but is a sweetheart.

What business mistake have you made that you will not repeat?
Not following my instincts. If something doesn't feel right, it probably isn't.

How do you spend your free time?
With my amazing family and friends.

Where is your favorite place to go with your girlfriends?
Anywhere we can escape, catch up, give advice, vent and laugh.

SCHIFFMAN CREATIVE

212.879.1006
schiffmancreative.com

Imaginative. Savvy. Dedicated.
Schiffman Creative is one of New York's most dynamic boutique graphic design
and creative consulting agencies. Operating from Manhattan's Upper East Side,
Erin and Philip Schiffman have secured their place among the sought-after
creative teams in New York City by developing lasting relationships and
delivering proven results. Schiffman Creative can help your brand achieve
visual excellence without compromising your own unique identity.

Photos by E. Leigh Photography

SEX ED SOLUTIONS

49 W 24th St, 8th Floor, New York, 212.686.5359
sexedsolutions.com, igniteyourpleasure.com

Engaging. Inspiring. Empowering.
As a nationally recognized certified sexuality expert, Amy Levine is featured in many well-known magazines including *Cosmopolitan*, *Glamour*, *Health* and *SELF*. In her private coaching sessions and group workshops, Amy answers all your sexuality questions and solves your most intimate sexual dilemmas. Ultimately, inspiring you—whether single or coupled—to become savvy and empowered in and out of the bedroom.

Amy Levine, MA, CSE

Q&A

What are your most popular products or services?
My coaching sessions and workshops—especially those for bachelorette parties and girls'-night-out soirées that include tidbits, tips and tricks.

People may be surprised to know...
I'm the real deal—I have my master's degree in human sexuality from NYU and certification from AASECT.

What or who inspired you to start your business?
Wanting women and men to learn about sexuality in a fun, educational and honest way, so they become sexually confident and satisfied!

What is your indulgence?
Pleasure—whether it comes from great food, great shopping or great sex!

SKIN BY KYRA

By appointment only: 417 Grand St, New York, 917.609.6000
skinbykyra.com, Twitter: @kyralive

Radiant. Peaceful. Welcoming.
Skin by Kyra is a sanctuary for beauty and health tucked into a Lower East Side
residence. You can find many services that are deeply relaxing and will even
soothe away your wrinkles. Kyra's treatments are inspired by Indian and Asian
traditions and vitalized with modern science; they really work wonders. You can
also pick up great handmade skin-care products with exotic essential oils.

Photos by Emily DeVan Photography

Kyra Saulnier

Q&A

What are your most popular products or services?
My Ayurvedic Face and Body Rejuvenation is the most requested treatment and my Skin Polish is the best-selling product. Skin Polish was my first!

What tip would you give women who are starting a business?
Develop your intuition and then listen to it. If you believe in your ideas, you can succeed; stick with it, don't let others dissuade you.

What motivates you on a daily basis?
Feedback from my clients. Recently one said "If everyone could have a treatment with you, Kyra, there would be no more war." Enough said.

What is your motto or theme song?
Create balance in health and life, from the outside in.

Francine Rivera

Q&A

What are your most popular products or services?
Our amazing walnut polisher. It's a very fine grain, foaming, face and body polisher that leaves the skin unbelievably soft.

What motivates you on a daily basis?
Expression. I love expressing myself through my products, designs and concepts. I truly enjoy providing outstanding customer service. It's something I was born to do.

How do you relax?
I take a long, hot bubble bath. Nothing relaxes me more!

What place inspires you and why?
New York! No place is more inspirational, artful and upbeat. This city is amazing.

SOAPOLOGY

67 8th Ave, New York, 212.255.SOAP (7627)
Limelight Marketplace, 656 Avenue of Americas, New York, 212.255.SOAP (7627)
soapologynyc.com

Natural. Colorful. Aromatic.
Soapology is an all-natural skin-care company located in the fabulous
Meatpacking District in Manhattan. What is most unique about Soapology is
their aromatic oil bar where clients can choose or create a scent, which is then
blended into any product in the store. Try their wonderful hand treatment at
the vintage claw-foot bathtub. We guarantee your skin never felt so soft!

Photos by Emily DeWan Photography

West Village

Photos by Sofia Negron Photography, except portrait by Ryan Estes

SOFIA NEGRON PHOTOGRAPHY

917.975.6167
sofianegron.com, Twitter: @sofianegron

Authentic. Elegant. Connected.

New York City photographer Sofia Negron loves getting to know her couples. Sofia's easygoing manner and unobtrusive style puts everyone at ease and allows for more authentic imagery and fun. Sofia draws upon her experience as a professional dancer: anticipating the next moment and creating an image that responds to what is happening and draws you in. Sofia also photographs dance and actors' head shots.

Sofia
Negron

 # Q&A

What are your most popular products or services?
Couples love the New York Love Affair sessions. These are lifestyle portrait sessions designed to reflect a couples' love affair with each other and the city they live in.

What tip would you give women who are starting a business?
Believe in what you are doing, create a good support network and keep going. When things get bumpy, your belief in yourself is sometimes all you have.

What do you like best about owning a business?
I love getting to know my clients and building authentic relationships with them and the other businesses that help create the client's big day.

Tory Johnson

What tip would you give women
who are starting a business?
It's all about the hustle—the daily decisions
you make and actions you take. It doesn't
matter how fabulous your idea is if you
don't know to market and sell it.

What motivates you on a daily basis?
Emails and calls from women nationwide
who are determined to make tomorrow
better than yesterday—and they're willing
to do the hard work to make it happen.

How do you relax?
Playing Scrabble and shopping sprees at
Target with my husband and our kids.

What do you CRAVE?
My purpose is to fuel the success of the
women I serve, so I cheer relentlessly
for their victories big and small.

SPARK & HUSTLE

212.290.2600
sparkandhustle.com, Twitter: @toryjohnson

Curious. Daring. Transformational.
Tory Johnson's Spark & Hustle conferences provide tools to enable small
business owners to launch and grow their entrepreneurial dreams now. Profit
Partner programs deliver customized feedback and direction through intensive
coaching and business support. Participants value the "real deal" aspect
of Spark & Hustle: no upselling, no gimmicks, no tricks. Just nuts and bolts
advice on how to make more money through genuine business growth.

SPiN NEW YORK

48 E 23rd St, New York, 212.982.8802
spingalactic.com, Twitter: @SPiNgalactic

Innovative. Action-packed. Fun.
SPiN New York has taken the city's social scene by storm with a mix of sport,
design and entertainment since its launch in 2009. SPiN was created by Academy
Award–winning actress Susan Sarandon, Franck Raharinosy, Andrew Gordon,
Jonathan Bricklin, and designed by renowned designer Todd Oldham. The club
boasts a 13,000 sq. ft. space with up to 16 courts, a full bar, a restaurant, and
a private room. SPiN is open to members and guests alike for nightly events,
tournaments, private or group instruction, and casual socializing and play.

Susan Sarandon

Q&A

What are your most popular products or services?
The Dirty Dozen—weekly professional ping pong tournaments held on Fridays with a DJ, two MCs and a dance-off! Our tongue-in-cheek "Balls Are My Business" T-shirts and Inocente Tequila (it's smooth and delicious!). And ping pong, of course!

What inspired you to start your business?
We're still trying to figure that one out...

People would be surprised to know...
Susan can be seen at SPiN almost every Friday (schedule allowing) for our most exciting weekly tournament: The Dirty Dozen! As it is a tournament reserved for our cream of the crop players, she lets the pros play—but she's got a pretty great serve of her own!

Ger-Nis International photographed by
Emily DeWan Photography

What place inspires you and why?

> *My hometown, NYC, never ceases to inspire me. NYC is energized by people from all over the world who come here in pursuit of a dream.*

Wanda Mann of The Black Dress Traveler

Main photo courtesy of boutier, lower left photo courtesy of CCSkye, lower middle photo courtesy of Katherine Kwei, lower right photo courtesy of Rebecca Minkoff, portrait by Joanne Schulter Photography

STEFANIBAGS.COM

877.357.0707
StefaniBags.com, Twitter: @StefaniBags.com

Chic. Modern. Lust-worthy.

StefaniBags was developed to fill a growing demand for the freshest, coolest handbag designers online. The site offers the convenience of shopping at home in a stylish boutique setting. StefaniBags is a well-edited e-boutique that offers highly coveted, contemporary handbag, shoe and accessory brands that are chic and modern. The e-boutique's customer base has grown in the United States and around the globe.

Monica Prestia

Q&A

What are your most popular products or services?
Handbags of course!

What tip would you give women who are starting a business?
You must love what you are doing to succeed. Never give up, don't stop trying!

What do you like best about owning a business?
Making my own decisions and choices.

What is your motto or theme song?
Rocky song! Work harder, play harder!

What place inspires you and why?
Buenos Aires, where I was born, is filled with glamour, passion for life and the arts. Also, NYC, where I was raised. It is the city where all your dreams can come true.

Laura Siner

 Q&A

What are your most popular products or services?
Our rich fudge brownies in all shapes, sizes and flavors.

People may be surprised to know...
Sweet Muse brownies began as an activity to help prepare before acting in the theater at night.

What business mistake have you made that you will not repeat?
Underestimating the amount of extra help needed during the busy end-of-year holiday season.

How do you spend your free time?
Movies, theater, reading, walking in the park and (even still) baking.

SWEET MUSE

212.874.2801
sweetmuse.com, Twitter: @sweetmuse

Delicious. Delightful. Creative.
Sweet Muse bake shop specializes in rich fudge brownies baked to
order from scratch with premium ingredients and carefully wrapped
in gift tins and boxes to create customized personal and corporate
gifts. Sweet Muse can offer sweet inspiration for birthdays, weddings,
bridal showers, corporate events and other special occasions.

Sarah Endline

Q&A

What are your most popular products or services?
sweetriot's original bite-sized 100 percent dark chocolate "peaces" (cacao nibs) dunked in dark chocolate and packaged in reusable, recyclable tins that feature original artwork by emerging artists. Plus there is only one calorie per "peace."

People may be surprised to know...
Dark chocolate really comes from fruit– the cacao fruit. It is often compared with other superfoods and, in fact, there are many antioxidant charts that show the power of cacao is stronger than blueberries and red wine!

What do you CRAVE? In business? In life?
I crave exploration of new, amazing places and people!

SWEETRIOT

212.431.7468
sweetriot.com, Twitter: @sweetriot

Innovative. Colorful. Yummy.
sweetriot is a chocolate company that is creating a sweet movement to fix the world!
sweetriot sources exclusively from farmers in Latin America, puts original artwork
by emerging artists on every package and celebrates culture and diversity along
the way. sweetriot uses all-natural, healthy ingredients that are antioxidant-packed
and only one calorie per "peace." Sweet for the world and sweet for you!

Photos by Jean-luc Mège

Main, lower left and middle photos by Brian Dorsey Studios, lower right photo by R Wagner Photography, portrait by Jen Huang Photography

TAMMY GOLSON EVENTS

917.860.3312
tammygolson.com, Twitter: @tammygolson

Artistic. Visionary. Resourceful.
Tammy Golson's sophisticated yet thoughtful approach to planning weddings and events is appreciated by her clients. She prides herself on being resourceful while assisting individuals in personalizing their events in creative, savvy and culinary-inspired ways. Tammy Golson Events helps those who want to treat their guests to an event that marks the milestone with delicious, well-prepared and beautifully presented cuisine.

 Q&A

What are your most popular products or services?
Full wedding and event planning, partial planning and day-of coordination. I love planning bridal and baby showers and kids' birthday parties as well.

What do you like best about owning a business?
I love helping people mark their most important milestones in a way that suits them best. Each client and event brings amazing variety to my business, which I welcome wholeheartedly.

What place inspires you and why?
New York City brings out the very best in me. I am surrounded by talent, delicious food, smart and interesting people. I am always encouraged to strive to do better.

Tammy Golson

TASTE BUDS

109 W 27th St, 10th Floor, New York, 212.242.2248
tastebudscook.com, Twitter: @tastebudscook

Creative. Engaging. Delicious.

Jessi Walter, a former VP on Wall Street, turned in her calculator for a spatula when she founded Taste Buds (formerly Cupcake Kids!). Based out of the only kids' kitchen studio in Manhattan, Taste Buds offers an ever-growing variety of hands-on cooking classes for kids, moms and families including weekly classes, camps, birthday parties, school field trips and more. Experience a fun and unique culinary adventure with family and friends.

Photos by E. Leigh Photography

Jessi Walter

Q&A

What are your most popular products or services?
Cooking birthday parties, special holiday classes, and mommy and me classes.

People may be surprised to know...
I'm over six feet tall and was a tall model on the Martha Stewart Show. Martha also came to one of our birthday parties, which was a real treat.

What business mistake have you made that you will not repeat?
Taking too long to make decisions. Keep moving forward!

How do you spend your free time?
Relaxing with family and friends, trying new restaurants and baking cookies.

What is your indulgence?
Cookie dough.

Chelsea

TRACY ANDERSON METHOD STUDIO

408 Greenwich St, 3rd Floor, New York, 212.965.1408
tracyandersonmethod.com

Empowering. Transformational. Inventive.
Tracy Anderson's New York studio, located in TriBeCa, offers both membership and private training options. Members participate in group classes that range in focus from muscular structure–based classes to dance/aerobic/cardio-based. The classes are held in the main room where resistance band systems line the ceiling. Highly skilled Tracy Anderson Method trainers lead clients through their individualized programs that are designed to activate smaller muscle groups and that also incorporate Tracy's customized hybrid reformer, ballet barres and hanging cubes.

Tracy Anderson

Q&A

What are your most popular products or services?
I have a successful line of DVDs that reaches a global audience.

What tip would you give women who are starting a business?
Only weigh in on the things that you really know what you're talking about; stick to your strengths.

Who is your role model or mentor?
My mother, Diana. She taught me the importance of being honest and following your passion. She is secure, confident, creative, and gave me all the elements I need.

What is your biggest fear?
Not being able to create anymore or not being able to bring anything new and inspiring to the business.

TriBeCa

Martha Desbiens and
Kristi Stromberg Wright

Q&A

What are your most popular products or services?
We're most often asked to design roof terraces or backyard gardens but greenroofs and living walls are really taking off.

People may be surprised to know...
New York City offers a tax credit for installing a greenroof.

Who is your role model or mentor?
We both have young children, and their inquisitiveness and creativity inspires us every day.

What business mistake have you made that you will not repeat?
We've been too shy about telling people how excited we are about the work we're doing.

What is your indulgence?
Stopping for chocolate ice cream between meetings.

Where is your favorite place to go with your girlfriends?
Out for a really delicious meal or coffee. Good food is key, but the most important part is the company.

What do you CRAVE? In business? In life?
Creating beautiful moments that make you stop and wonder.

VERTNY, INC.

212.799.1716
vertny.com

Modern. Fresh. Green.

VertNY, inc. is a landscape design firm specializing in the integration of innovative, sustainable techniques with attractive, inviting designs for the urban landscape. The principals of the firm, Kristi Stromberg Wright and Martha Desbiens, have collaborated on numerous residential, corporate and public landscape projects, including roof terraces, backyard gardens, estates, public plazas, greenroofs and living walls.

WGIRLS INC

233 W 15th St, Ste 2W, Manhattan, 888-WGIRLS8 (888.944.7578)
wgirls.org, Twitter: @wgirlsinc

Philanthropic. Fun. Rewarding.

Touted by the *Wall Street Journal* as perfecting the model for making philanthropy fun, social and transparent to the next generation of donors, WGIRLS is an all-female volunteer organization working to provide underprivileged women and children with the resources necessary to lead healthy, productive and successful lives. Founded in 2007 and headquartered in Manhattan, WGIRLS is now a global organization.

Amy Elizabeth Heller

 # Q&A

What are your most popular
products or services?
The WGIRLS are best known for their
wildly successful fund-raising events,
which routinely attract hundreds of young
professionals in cities across the country.

What tip would you give women
who are starting a business?
Trust your intuition and surround
yourself with strong, smart, ambitious
people who will keep you motivated,
challenged and in check!

What motivates you on a daily basis?
Knowing that our work is not only
making a difference in the lives of
thousands of people in need but also
enhancing the lives of our members.

Michelle Ward

Q&A

What tip would you give women who are starting a business?
Baby steps are underrated! Doing something small every day still gets you where you wanna go, and I'm convinced it's the best route to get there.

What do you like best about owning a business?
I love not having to hide my quirky self because it's "unprofessional." Nobody's telling me I can't have blue nails or say "crapballs," which is the sweetest kind of freedom.

What place inspires you and why?
My Brooklyn apartment! We have views from almost every room of the Manhattan Bridge, the Empire State Building and the Chrysler Building. It makes everything feel possible!

Who is your role model or mentor?
My mom. She lives life solely by her values, which is exactly what I aspire to. Also, she often gets mistaken for my sister. I hope I have her genes!

What do you CRAVE?
Relationships. Passion. Connection. Belly laughs. Forward movement. Partners in crime. Sweet potato fries. A fashion line by Punky Brewster. Witnessing someone discovering their grown-up dreams and realizing that it's possible.

WHEN I GROW UP COACH

917.678.7461
whenigrowupcoach.com, Twitter: @WhenIGroUpCoach

Spunky. Creative. Enthusiastic.

Michelle Ward helps creative people devise the career they think they can't have—or discover it to begin with! A certified life coach and an actress with a BFA from NYU, Michelle uses a dose of empathy, a shot of butt-kickin', a wagon-full of enthusiasm and a load of inspiration to help turn her clients' grown-up skills and values into a real-life career.

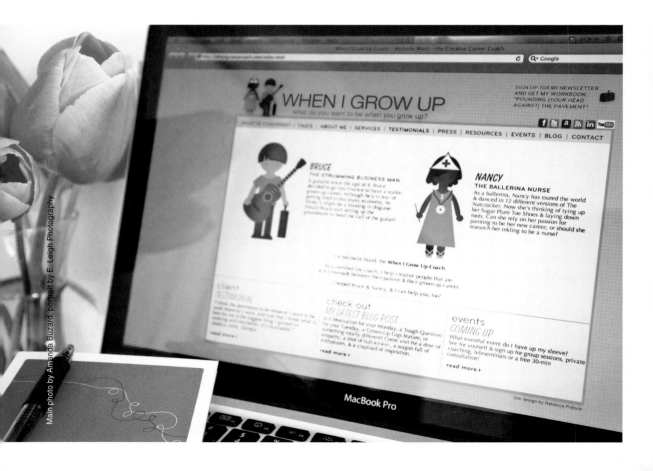

WIREMEDIA COMMUNICATIONS

212.686.1486
wiremedia.net, Twitter: @wiremedia

Strategic. Experienced. Detail-oriented.
WireMedia develops communications strategies for nonprofits and socially responsible businesses that improve lives, communities and environments. WireMedia's award-winning work has helped win advocacy efforts and campaigns, establish new businesses and grow existing organizations. Founded in New York City in 2002, the company has since expanded to Los Angeles, and works with a distinctive list of clients in major cities across the country.

Marcy Rye

 Q&A

What are your most popular
products or services?
Branding (logo design and identity collateral)
and online strategy (website design and
development, ads, social networking).

What tip would you give women
who are starting a business?
Have a solid plan and know where
you want to be by the end of year two.
It's not easy, but don't give up!

What do you like best about
owning a business?
I like the problem-solving aspect—the
satisfaction of providing solutions for
clients that really help them out.

How do you relax?
Biking, hiking, swimming, Tae Kwon Do,
wine tasting, travel, painting,
reading, playing with my cats...

THE YINOVA CENTER

74 E 11th St, New York, 212.533.2255
yinovacenter.com, Twitter: @yinova

Healing. Compassionate. Comforting.
Founded more than a decade ago by acupuncturist, herbalist and author Jill Blakeway,
The YinOva Center uses traditional Chinese medicine to treat modern families for a
wide variety of ailments. As the business grew, Jill's husband, Noah, joined her and in
2005 the *New York Times* named them as NY's best acupuncturists. The center now
has 19 treatment rooms and employs nine experienced and caring practitioners.

Photos by Belathée Photography

Jill Blakeway

Q&A

What tip would you give women who are starting a business?
Never forget that your customers have a choice. At The YinOva Center, we go the extra mile for each and every person who comes through our door.

What do you like best about owning a business?
I get enormous satisfaction from watching our center grow, and enjoy the creativity of dreaming about what we'll do next and then seeing those dreams become a reality.

How do you relax?
I plant fruits and vegetables in our garden in upstate New York and watch them grow. I love cooking with my husband and like feeding friends homegrown produce.

Index

By Category

By Category

By Neighborhood

By Neighborhood

Contributors

We believe in acknowledging, celebrating and passionately supporting locally owned businesses and entrepreneurs. We are extremely grateful to all contributors for this publication.

CRAVE Founder

Melody Biringer connects women in innovative ways so they can help each other pursue the lives they crave, in business and in pleasure.

thecravecompany.com
startupjunkie.com

MELODY BIRINGER

Innovative. Feminine. Connections.

Melody Biringer, self-avowed "start-up junkie," has built companies that range from Biringer Farm, a family-run specialty-food business, to home furnishings to a fitness studio.

Her current entrepreneurial love-child is The CRAVE Company, a network of businesses designed to creatively connect entrepreneurs who approach business in a fresh new way with the stylish consumers they desire. The CRAVE family includes CRAVEparty, CRAVEguides and CRAVEbusiness. What started out as girlfriends getting together for exclusive glam-gal gatherings, CRAVEparty has since expanded into CRAVEbusiness, a resource for entrepreneurs seeking a modern approach, and CRAVEguides, delivering style and substance. Since initially launching in Seattle, Melody has taken CRAVE to more than 19 US cities, including New York City, Boston, Los Angeles and Chicago, and internationally to cities such as Amsterdam and Toronto.

Melody is a loyal community supporter, versed traveler and strong advocate for women-owned businesses.

CRAVE NYC Partner

212.781.6390, curtainupevents.com
Twitter: @curtainupevents

DANIELLE BOBISH

Innovative. Savvy. Chic.

As founder and creative director of Curtain Up Events (CUE), Danielle plans, designs and coordinates weddings and events throughout NYC and the surrounding regions. Danielle founded CUE with the idea of injecting into the event industry a bit of the drama and artistry of theater. As a graduate of the University of Hartford's Hartt School of Music, Danielle's unique creative vision is derived in part from her former career as a professional actress performing on stages from Broadway to Bremerton. CUE has been honored with Best of Weddings 2011 on the Knot and is a two-time winner of the Bride's Choice Award on WeddingWire.

Danielle is excited to continue forging unexpected connections with CRAVE while establishing CRAVE NYC as the savvy businesswoman's go-to resource for all that is authentically New York.

INNA SHAMIS

CRAVE NYC Partner
inna@agcomgroup.com
Twitter: @agcg, agcomgroup.com

Passionate. Vivacious. Innovative.

Inna Shamis is a seasoned communications specialist with over 15 years' experience in PR, marketing and client management, working with some of the world's most recognized brands. With a career that began in the mid-1990s, her widespread background spans a number of industries and she maintains extensive global contacts in the media and entertainment, consumer, beauty and wellness, travel and hospitality, and lifestyle sectors.

Following a formative career in corporate America, Inna founded AvantGarde Communications Group, a full-service firm that delivers expertise in PR, marketing, business development, copywriting and creative solutions. With the help of her cultivated background and depth of experience, the firm delivers innovative ideas, sharp execution and powerful results.

SARAH STANTON

CRAVE NYC Partner
sarahs@craveparty.com

Curious. Inventive. Zealous.

Sarah Stanton is a native Michigander who stepped foot in the concrete jungle for what was supposed to be a six-month internship. Six years later she now considers herself an honorary New Yorker.

The constant change in NYC keeps Sarah motivated to come up with fresh ideas, stay plugged-in and get involved! Known by her friends as fearless, filled with random facts, an expert on local spots and the girl who can talk to anyone, teaming with CRAVE was a no-brainer.

"The women I've met, tips I've learned, resources shared and partnerships/friendships I've built are priceless. I'm absolutely thrilled to have my name on this fantastic publication and I'm proud to say that CRAVE marked the beginning of my journey as an entrepreneur."

Contributors

Headquarters

Alison Turner
graphic designer
alisonjturner.com

Alison is a passionate designer and critical thinker from Seattle. She supports human rights and the local food movement. She enjoys researching interesting things, volunteering, being outside, dancing, cooking and running.

Amanda Buzard
lead designer
amandabuzard.com

Amanda is a Seattle native inspired by clean patterns and vintage design. She chases many creative and active pursuits in her spare time, including photography, baking, attempting DIY projects and exploring the beautiful Pacific Northwest.

Lilla Kovacs
operations manager
lilla@thecravecompany.com

As the operations manager, Lilla ensures that everything runs like clockwork. In her limited spare time, she enjoys baking, shoe shopping, traveling, art, Apple products and daydreaming about her hometowns, Arad, Romania and Tel-Aviv, Israel.

Nicole Shema
project manager
nicole@thecravecompany.com

A Seattle native, Nicole is happy to be back in her city after graduating from the University of Oregon in 2009. Nicole has a passion for travel and she loves discovering new places around Seattle with friends, running, shopping, and reading in coffee shops.

Carrie Wicks
copy editor
linkedin.com/in/carriewicks

Carrie has been proofreading professionally for 14-plus years in mostly creative fields. When she's not proofreading or copyediting, she's reading, singing jazz, walking in the woods or gardening.

Celine Baldevia
design intern
celine@thecravecompany.com

Celine spent her middle and high school years on a US military base in South Korea before moving to Seattle to study digital design at Seattle University. She enjoys playing sports, drawing, traveling and discovering new things.

NYC Team

Emily McCollum
intern
emily@emilygracedesign.com
352.897.0542
Twitter: @emgracedesign
@emilygrace514

While working on the CRAVEguide, Emily held the position of associate planner for Curtain Up Events. She has since moved to Florida where she continues to produce events with her company, Emily Grace Design.

Jacqueline Mayers
intern
JacquelineMayers@hotmail.com
Twitter: @JackieMayers

As a recent grad who got her bachelor's in mass media, arts and journalism, Jacqueline is hoping to work for a public relations agency or a nonprofit.

Kiki Suhadi
intern
Kiki Suhadi is a student in NYC and an associate planner for Curtain Up Events.

A. Anaiz Photography
photographer
aanaizphotography.com
Twitter: @AAnaizPhoto
917.275.3468
info@aanaizphotography.com

Amy Anaiz is a self-taught New York and Florida–based wedding and portrait photographer with a contemporary eye. Her goal is to make sure that each session is more like a casual journey through each frame captured.

Belathée Photography
photographer
917.783.3207, belathee.com
Twitter: @belathee

Combining a romantic, timeless quality with a modern, fresh and wonderfully inventive perspective, Annabel and Dorothée love to tell a story through photography.

E. Leigh Photography
photographer
eleigh.com, 646.468.8530
Twitter: eleighphoto

Erin Leigh is a lifestyle and wedding photographer based in New York City, but available for assignments everywhere.

Contributors (continued)

NYC Team (continued)

Emily DeWan
photographer
emilydewan.com
Twitter: @emilydewan
917.620.5111

Emily loves working with people to create personality-driven portraits and capturing beautiful moments of weddings. When not behind the camera, she enjoying cycling through NYC and swing dancing.

Jen Huang Photography
photographer
347.323.5736
JenHuangPhotography.com
JenHuangBlog.com

Jen Huang is a fine-art wedding and portrait photographer specializing in light-filled, romantic images for the society bride. Her work is exemplified in her continued dedication to film.

Missy Photography
photographer
missyphotography.com
Twitter: @MissyPhoto
619.985.1767

Melissa Murphy is a published NYC photographer with skills honed in the Southern California sunshine, specializing in weddings and portraiture. She is an avid fan of all things lovely.

Sofia Negron
photographer
sofianegron.com
sofianegronblog.com
Twitter: @sofianegron
917.975.6167

A former professional dancer, Sofia Negron loves capturing energy and movement. Sofia not only tells authentic love stories through her wedding photography, but also photographs dancers and other artists.

Special thanks to our additional contributors:
Iris Bachman, Taka Kawachi, Tanzie Johnson and Tracy Toler

Craving Savings

Get the savings you crave with the following participating businesses—one time only!

☐ Astrostyle.com
20% discount

☐ Babeland
10% discount

☐ Belathée Photography
10% discount

☐ Bump Brooklyn
15% discount

☐ Bundle Children's Boutique
20% discount

☐ Carli Beardsley Atelier
50% discount

☐ Causey Contemporary
10% discount

☐ Center Of Female Empowerment
10% discount

☐ City Treehouse
10% discount

☐ Color Our World
20% discount

☐ Curious Light
10% discount

☐ The Decorista
15% discount

☐ DM Events
20% discount

☐ Elizabeth Charles
10% discount

☐ Elke Von Freudenberg
10% discount

☐ Emily DeWan Photography, Inc.
25% discount

☐ Footzyrolls
15% discount

☐ Friends Of Jodi
50% discount

☐ Global Fashion Brands
20% discount

☐ Goji Gourmet
10% discount

☐ Gotham Organizers
15% discount

☐ Healthy Wealthy & Smart radio show
20% discount

☐ Helen Julia New York
10% discount

☐ Her Journey
20% discount

☐ InStep Consulting
10% discount

☐ Jan Consulting Group, LLP
20% discount

☐ Jen Huang Photography
50% discount

☐ Jillian Wright Clinical Skin Spa
10% discount

☐ Journelle
15% discount

☐ Karen Litzy, MSPT Physical Therapist
20% discount

☐ les Egoistes Creative Services
20% discount

☐ LuxuryMonograms.com
10% discount

☐ Merci New York
10% discount

☐ Nail Taxi NYC
10% discount

☐ NIARA Consulting
50% discount

☐ One Life, Live-It, Inc.
10% discount

☐ OrganizeNY
10% discount

☐ Pawfect Day
50% discount

Craving Savings

- [ ] Pins & Needles
  10% discount
- [ ] 'PRENEUR
  10% discount
- [ ] pūr~lisse beauty
  10% discount
- [ ] purely elizabeth
  20% discount
- [ ] The Re-Stylist
  20% discount
- [ ] Real Nutrition NYC
  10% discount
- [ ] Rebecca Luke Style
  20% discount
- [ ] Soapology
  15% discount
- [ ] StefaniBags.com
  20% discount
- [ ] sweetriot
  20% discount
- [ ] Tammy Golson Events
  15% discount
- [ ] Taste Buds
  10% discount
- [ ] When I Grow Up Coach
  20% discount
- [ ] WireMedia Communications
  10% discount

Use code CRAVE for online discount

Details of discounts may vary from business to business, so please call first.
The CRAVE company shall not be held responsible for variations on discounts at
individual businesses. This page may not be photocopied or otherwise duplicated.